DESIGNS FOR ADULT LEARNING

Practical resources, exercises, and course outlines from the father of adult learning.

MALCOLM S. KNOWLES

ASTD
AMERICAN SOCIETY
FOR TRAINING AND
DEVELOPMENT

Ordering information: Books published by the American Society for Training and Development can be ordered by calling 703/683-8100.

Library of Congress Catalog Card Number: 95-083164

ISBN: 1-56286-025-9

ASTD

AMERICAN SOCIETY
FOR TRAINING AND
DEVELOPMENT

1640 KING STREET
BOX 1443
ALEXANDRIA, VIRGINIA
22313-2043

703/683-8100
FAX 703/683-8103

Table of Contents

Preface

I retired as professor of adult and community college education at North Carolina State University in 1979 after five years there. Previously, I had been a professor of education at Boston University for 14 years; executive director of the Adult Education Association of the United States for eight years; director of adult education at the YMCAs of Detroit, Chicago, and Boston for 10 years; and director of training for the National Youth Administration of Massachusetts for six years.

During this time, I also conducted short courses, workshops, and conference sessions for a variety of institutions and organizations, including colleges and universities, government agencies, voluntary organizations, businesses, and religious institutions in this country and abroad. After retirement, I continued to perform these activities as well as write books and articles full-time.

My first book, *Informal Adult Education*, was published in 1950, and my latest, *The Making of an Adult Educator*, in 1989. I have published 17 books—two of them coauthored with my wife—and have published 230 articles.

Recently one of my publishers asked me, "Malcolm, is there anything you have wanted to say that you haven't said yet?" My first reaction was, "Of course not." But I started thinking seriously about that question, and it gradually dawned on me that I have experimented with a number of designs in my courses, workshops, and conference sessions, that I have copies of most of them, and that it might be useful to others for me to analyze and share them. This book is the fruit of that process.

CHAPTER 1

Conceptual Foundations

The designs in this book are based on two conceptual foundations: learning theory and design theory.

Learning Theory: The Andragogical Model Versus the Pedagogical Model

Since the Middle Ages, the pedagogical model has served as the foundation of traditional education. In fact, it is the only way of thinking about education that most people know, because it is what they experience in school. The following assumptions about learners are inherent in the pedagogical model:

- **Concept of the learner.** The learner is a dependent personality by definition, because the pedagogical model assigns to the teacher full responsibility for making all the decisions about what should be learned, when it should be learned, how it should be learned, and whether it has been learned. The only task for the learner, therefore, is to submissively carry out the teacher's directions.
- **Role of the learner's experience.** Learners enter into an educational activity with little experience to use as a resource for learning. It is the experience of the teachers, the textbook author, and the audiovisual aids producer that counts. Accordingly, the backbone of the pedagogical methodology is transmission techniques—lectures, assigned readings, and audiovisual presentations.
- **Readiness to learn.** Students become ready to learn when they are told they have to learn if they want to advance to the next grade. This readiness is largely a function of age.
- **Orientation to learning.** Students enter into an educational activity with a subject-centered orientation to learning. They see learning as a process of acquiring prescribed subject-matter content. Consequently, the curriculum is organized according to content units and is sequenced according to the logic of the subject matter.
- **Motivation to learn.** External pressures from teachers and par-

ents, competition for grades, and the consequences of failure are the students' primary motivations.

In contrast—and in equally pure form—the following assumptions about learners are inherent in the andragogical model:

▶ **Concept of the learner.** As adults, we have a deep psychological need to be self-directing—to be perceived by others and treated by others as able to take responsibility for ourselves. When we find ourselves in situations where we feel others imposing their wills on us without our participation in making decisions that affect us, we feel resentment and resistance.

▶ **Role of the learner's experience.** The andragogical model assumes that adults enter into an educational activity with a greater volume and a different quality of experience than youths. The greater volume is obvious—the longer we live, the more experience we accumulate. The difference in quality of experience arises from the different roles adults and young people perform.

This difference in experience affects the planning and conducting of an educational activity. First, it means that adults are themselves the richest learning resource for one another for many kinds of learning. Hence, the greater emphasis in adult education is on such techniques as group discussion, simulation exercises, laboratory experiences, field experiences, problem-solving projects, and interactive media.

The differences in experience also assume greater heterogeneity in groups of adults. The range of experience in a group of adults of various ages will be greater than that in a group of same-aged youths. Consequently, adult education emphasizes individualized learning plans, such as learning contracts.

Readiness To Learn

The andragogical model assumes that adults become ready to learn when they experience a need to know or be able to do something to perform more effectively in some aspect of their lives. Among the chief sources of readiness are the developmental tasks associated with moving from one stage of development to another. Any change—marriage, the birth of children, the loss of a job, divorce, the death of a friend or relative, or a change of residence—can trigger a readiness to learn. But we don't need to wait for readiness to develop naturally. We can induce readiness by exposing learners to more effective role models, engaging them in career planning, and providing them with diagnostic experiences to assess the gaps between where they are now and where they want and need to be in terms of their personal competencies.

Orientation to Learning

Because adults are motivated to learn after they experience a need, they enter an educational activity with a life-, task-, or problem-centered orientation to learning. The chief implication of this assumption is the importance of organizing learning experiences (i.e., the curriculum) around life situations, rather than according to subject-matter units. For example, courses that are called Composition I, Composition II, and Composition III in high school might better be called Writing Better Business Letters, Writing for Pleasure and Profit, and Improving Your Professional Communications in an adult education program.

Motivation To Learn

Although the andragogical model acknowledges that adults will respond to some external motivators—for example, a chance for promotion, a change of jobs, or a change in technology—it proposes that the more potent motivators are internal—such as self-esteem, recognition by peers, better quality of life, greater self-confidence, self-actualization, and so on. Program announcements should emphasize these kinds of benefits.

Conclusion

As I have asserted in several books and many articles, I regard the pedagogical and andragogical models as parallel, not antithetical. It is the responsibility of the educator to check out which assumptions of the two models are realistic for a given situation. In some situations, such as when learners are experiencing a new and strange type of content or are confronting a machine they have never seen before, learners may be truly dependent on receiving some didactic instruction before they can initiate their own learning. In such situations, the pedagogical assumption of dependency is realistic, and pedagogical strategies are appropriate (at least up to the point that the learners have acquired sufficient background knowledge to start taking responsibility for their own learning). In many more situations, however, the andragogical strategies would be realistic from the outset.

Design Theory: Content Design Versus Process Design

The pedagogical and andragogical models employ two very different theoretical approaches to the design and operation of educational programs. The basic format of the pedagogical model is a *content design*, which requires the teacher to answer only four questions:

- **What content needs to be covered?** It is the teacher's responsibility to cover, through lectures or assigned readings, all of the content that the students need to learn. Thus, the teacher (or pedagogue) constructs a long list of items to be covered.
- **How can this content be organized into manageable units?** The pedagogue clusters the content into appropriate time units— say, 50-minute lesson plans or three-hour workshops.
- **What is the most logical sequence for presenting these units?** It is the logic of the subject matter, not the readiness of the learners or other psychological factors, that determines the sequence. In scientific or mathematical content programs, the sequence is from simple to complex; in history, it is chronological.
- **What is the most efficient means of transmitting this content?** In the case of highly conceptual content, the preferred means would be lecture or audiovisual presentations and assigned readings. If the content involves skill performance, the transmission means would be demonstration by the teacher and drill by the students.

In contrast, the basic format of the andragogical model is a *process design*. The andragogical model assigns dual roles to the facilitator of learning (a title preferred over "teacher"). First and most importantly, he or she designs and manages procedures that will facilitate the acquisition of content by the learners. Second, he or she will act as a content resource. The andragogical model assumes that many resources other than the teacher are available to learners. These resources include peers, people in the community with specialized knowledge and skills, material and media resources, and field experiences. One of the principal responsibilities of the facilitator is to know about these resources and to link learners with them. This process is often called *educational brokering*.

CHAPTER 2

Components of an Andragogical Process Design

An andragogical process design consists of eight components:
▶ preparing the learners for the program
▶ setting the climate
▶ involving learners in mutual planning
▶ involving learners in diagnosing their learning needs
▶ involving learners in forming their learning objectives
▶ involving learners in designing learning plans
▶ helping learners carry out their learning plans
▶ involving learners in evaluating their learning outcomes.

Preparing the Learners for the Program

The most common introduction of a program to potential learners is an announcement that describes the program's purpose, objectives, meeting time and place, audience, registration procedures, cost, and potential benefits. I like the announcement to say something about the participatory nature of the program design so the learners arrive with realistic expectations about how they will be involved. The announcement might also suggest things for them to think about, such as what special needs, questions, topics, and problems they hope the program will deal with. In some cases, registrants might be able to send this kind of information to the program planners before the event.

Setting the Climate

In my estimation, a climate conducive to learning is a prerequisite for effective learning. It seems tragic to me that so little attention is paid to climate in traditional education. Two aspects of climate are important: physical and psychological.

Physical Climate

The typical classroom setup, with chairs in rows and a lectern in front, is probably the one least conducive to learning that the fertile human brain could invent. It announces to anyone entering the room that the name of the game here is one-way transmission—that the proper role for the students is to sit and listen to the teacher. I make a point of getting to a meeting room well before the learners arrive. If it is set up like a classroom, I move the lectern to a corner and rearrange the chairs in one large circle or several small circles. I prefer to place the learners at tables of five or six. I also prefer bright and cheerful meeting rooms.

Psychological Climate

Important as physical climate is, psychological climate is even more important. The following characteristics create a psychological climate conducive to learning:

- **A climate of mutual respect.** People are more open to learning when they feel respected. If they feel that they are being talked down to, ignored, or regarded as incapable, or that their experience is not being valued, then their energy is spent dealing with these feelings at the expense of learning.
- **A climate of collaboration.** Because of their earlier school experiences where competition for grades and the teacher's favor was the norm, adults tend to enter into any educational activity with rivalry toward fellow learners. Because peers are often the richest resources for learning, this competitiveness makes these resources inaccessible. The climate-setting exercises that I open all my courses and workshops with put the learners into a sharing relationship from the beginning for this reason.
- **A climate of mutual trust.** People learn more from those they trust than from those they aren't sure they can trust. And here we, who are put in the position of teacher or trainer of adults, are at a disadvantage. Students in schools learn at an early age to regard teachers with suspicion until the teachers prove themselves to be trustworthy. Why? For one thing, they have power over students; they are authorized to give grades, to determine who passes or fails, and to hand out punishments and rewards. For another thing, the institutions in which they work present them in catalogues and program announcements as authority figures. In my courses and workshops, I present myself as a human being rather than as an authority figure; I trust people I work with and work to gain their trust.
- **A climate of support.** People learn better when they feel supported rather than judged or threatened. I try to convey my desire to be supportive by demonstrating my acceptance of them with an un-

qualified positive regard, empathizing with their problems or worries, and defining my role as that of helper. I also organize them into peer-support groups and coach them on how to support one another.

- **A climate of openness and authenticity.** When people feel free to say what they really think and feel, they are more willing to examine new ideas and risk new behaviors than when they feel defensive. If teachers or trainers demonstrate openness and authenticity in their own behavior, this will be the model that learners will want to adopt.

- **A climate of pleasure.** Learning should be one of the most pleasant and gratifying experiences in life; it is, after all, the way people can achieve their full potential. Learning should be an adventure, spiced with the excitement of discovery. It should be fun. I think that it is sad that so much of our previous educational experience was so dull.

- **A climate of humanness.** Perhaps what I have been saying about climate can be summed with the adjective *human*. Learning is a very human activity. The more people feel they are being treated as human beings, the more they are likely to learn. This means providing for human comfort—good lighting and ventilation, comfortable chairs, availability of refreshments, frequent breaks, and the like. It also means providing a caring, accepting, respecting, and helping social atmosphere.

Exhibit 2-1, "Basic Climate-Setting Exercise," outlines an exercise that I use in all my courses and workshops. It generally takes from 30 to 60 minutes.

Involving Learners in Mutual Planning

The andragogical process model emphasizes learners sharing the responsibility for planning learning activities with the facilitator. There is a basic law of human nature at work here. People tend to feel committed to any decision in proportion to the extent to which they have participated in making it. They tend to feel uncommitted to any decision that they feel others are making for or imposing on them.

In opening every program, I make clear that I am coming in with a *process plan*—a set of procedures for involving them in determining the content of their study. Learners need the security of knowing that I do have a plan, but even this process plan is open to their influence

In the following sections, I describe how I involve them as individuals or subgroups in diagnosing their learning needs, forming their objectives, planning and conducting their own learning activities, and evaluating their learning outcomes.

Diagnosing Their Own Learning Needs

At the very simplest level, learners can share in small groups what they perceive their needs and interests to be regarding the acquisition of knowledge or skill in a given content area. One member of each group can volunteer to summarize the results of this discussion. This way, the learners will at least enter into the learning experience with some awareness of what they would like to get out of it.

But you can induce a deeper and more specific level of awareness by having them engage in some sort of self-diagnostic exercise, using tools such as those presented in Figure 1, "Self-Diagnostic Rating Scale," and Figure 2, "Competency Diagnostic and Planning Guide."

The Remaining Components

To accomplish the remaining four components of the design process listed below, I use the magic of the learning contract:

> ▶ involving learners in forming their learning objectives
> ▶ involving learners in designing learning plans
> ▶ helping learners carry out their learning plans
> ▶ involving learners in evaluating their learning outcomes.

Learning contracts are the most effective way I know to help learners structure their learning. (Some people have difficulty with the term *contract* because of its legalistic flavor and substitute *learning plan* or *learning agreement*.) To help with this process, I provide learners with reprints of Exhibit 2-2, "Guidelines for Using Learning Contracts."

I use learning contracts in almost all of my practice. Students contract with me to meet the requirements of the university courses I teach. (Incidentally, even though there may be a number of nonnegotiable requirements in university courses, the means by which students accomplish the required objectives can be highly individualized.) Students going out on a field experience, such as a practicum or internship, contract with me and the field supervisor. I also use contracts in short-term workshops, with the contracts negotiated at the end of the workshop that specify how the students are going to continue to learn on their own. Finally, I use contracts in my in-service education programs. Many physicians, nurses, social workers, managers, teachers, and consultants use learning contracts for continuing personal and professional development.

Exercises

I occasionally use exercises, especially simulations and role plays, in my courses and workshops. A resource that I have found particularly useful in selecting appropriate exercises is Pfeiffer and Jones's *A Handbook of Structured Experiences for Human Relations Training* (University Associates, 1969).

One exercise that I use most frequently—indeed, whenever I am going to involve the learners in peer-review of self-diagnosed learning needs, learning contracts, and portfolios of evidence—is Exhibit 2-3, "Consultation Exercise."

In this chapter:

❖ Exhibit 2-1. Basic Climate-Setting Exercise ❖

After being introduced by the program chairperson, I explain that I see my role in this course or workshop to be twofold: first and foremost, as the designer and manager of a set of procedures for facilitating the participants' learning; and second, as a resource person with responsibility for sharing whatever content information I have that is relevant to their learning and making available to them information about other content resources.

My first responsibility as a facilitator is to create a climate conducive to learning. I ask participants to get into groups of four to six and share the following four things about themselves, with one member of each group volunteering to serve as a reporter to summarize the information for the larger group:

▶ **Their *whos*.** Who are they as unique human beings? I ask them to think of one thing about themselves that makes them different from everyone else in the room. As an example, I say that I am the only person in the room wearing an Indian bola tie—a habit I got into after receiving one as a token of appreciation from residents of a Navajo reservation where I had conducted a workshop.

▶ **Their *whats*.** What is their work experience, including their present position? I explain that I have been director of training for the National Youth Administration for Massachusetts; a director of adult education for the YMCAs of Boston, Detroit, and Chicago; a professor of adult education at Boston University and North Carolina State University; and that since I retired from North Carolina State in 1979 I have been busier than when I had a full-time job.

▶ **Their resources.** What special resources are they bringing into this activity that other learners should know about and tap into? For instance, I say that my special resource is an in-depth knowledge of the research and practice-oriented literature about adult learning in particular and adult education in general.

▶ **Their questions, problems, and concerns.** What issues do the learners hope to address by coming into this activity?

I suggest that the reporters take about 20 or 30 minutes getting this information from each member. I ask the reporters to keep their notes handy so they can identify any other issues at the end of the course. I usually close the exercise with a review of the characteristics of a climate conducive to learning that were spelled out earlier in Chapter 2.

Figure 1. Self-Diagnostic Rating Scale

Indicate on the six-point scale next to each of the competencies listed below:

▶ the *required* level for excellent performance of the role you are in now or are preparing for by placing an "R" (for required level) at the appropriate point

▶ the level of your present development of each competency by placing a "P" (for present level) at the appropriate point.

For example, if your role is that of teacher, you probably would place the Rs for the competencies for the role of learning facilitator higher than you would for the competencies for the role of administrator. You will emerge with a profile of the gaps between where you are now and where you need to be in order to perform your role well. Notice that room has been left for you to write in additional competencies.

This is how it would look:

		P			R
0	1	2	3	4	5
Absent	Low (aware of it)	Moderate (conceptual understanding)			High (expert)

AS A LEARNING FACILITATOR

The Theory of Adult Learning

1. Ability to describe and apply modern concepts and research findings regarding the needs, interests, motivations, capacities, and developmental characteristics of adults as learners

0	1	2	3	4	5

2. Ability to describe the differences in assumptions about youths and adults as learners and the implications of these differences for teaching

0	1	2	3	4	5

3. Ability to assess the forces on learners from the larger environment (i.e., groups, organizations, and cultures) and to manipulate them constructively

0	1	2	3	4	5

4. Ability to describe the various theories of learning and assess their relevance to particular adult learning situations

0	1	2	3	4	5

5. Ability to conceptualize and explain the role of teacher as a facilitator and resource person for self-directed learners

0	1	2	3	4	5

6. _____

0	1	2	3	4	5

Permission to reproduce and use this rating scale is granted without limitation. Reports of results would be appreciated. Send to Malcolm S. Knowles, 1923 East Joyce St., #231, Fayetteville, AR 72703.

Designing and Implementing Learning Experiences

1. Ability to describe the difference between a content plan and a process design

0   1   2   3   4   5

2. Ability to design learning experiences for a variety of purposes, taking into account individual differences among learners

0   1   2   3   4   5

3. Ability to engineer a physical and psychological climate of mutual respect, trust, openness, support, and safety

0   1   2   3   4   5

4. Ability to establish a warm, empathic, facilitative relationship with learners of all sorts

0   1   2   3   4   5

5. Ability to engage learners responsibly in self-diagnoses of needs for learning

0   1   2   3   4   5

6. Ability to engage learners in forming objectives that are meaningful to them

0   1   2   3   4   5

7. Ability to involve learners appropriately in the planning, conducting, and evaluating of learning activities

0   1   2   3   4   5

8. _____

0   1   2   3   4   5

Helping Learners Become Self-Directing

1. Ability to explain the conceptual difference between didactic instruction and self-directed learning

0   1   2   3   4   5

2. Ability to design and conduct one-hour, three-hour, one-day, and three-day learning experiences to develop the skills of self-directed learning

0   1   2   3   4   5

3. Ability to model the role of self-directed learning in your own behavior

0   1   2   3   4   5

4. _____

0   1   2   3   4   5

Selecting Methods, Techniques, and Materials

1. Ability to describe the range of methods or formats for organizing learning experiences

0   1   2   3   4   5

2. Ability to describe the range of techniques available for facilitating learning

0   1   2   3   4   5

3. Ability to identify the range of materials available as resources for learning

0   1   2   3   4   5

4. Ability to provide a rationale for selecting a particular method, technique, or material for achieving particular educational objectives

0   1   2   3   4   5

5. Ability to evaluate methods, techniques, and materials for their effectiveness in achieving particular educational outcomes

0	I	2	3	4	5

6. Ability to develop and manage procedures for the construction of competency models

0	I	2	3	4	5

7. Ability to construct and use tools and procedures for assessing competency-development needs

0	I	2	3	4	5

8. Ability to use a variety of presentation methods effectively

0	I	2	3	4	5

9. Ability to use a variety of experiential and simulation methods effectively

0	I	2	3	4	5

10. Ability to use audience-participation methods effectively

0	I	2	3	4	5

11. Ability to use group dynamics and small-group discussion techniques effectively

0	I	2	3	4	5

12. Ability to invent new techniques to fit new situations

0	I	2	3	4	5

13. Ability to evaluate learning outcomes and processes and to select or construct appropriate instruments and procedures for this purpose

0	I	2	3	4	5

14. Ability to confront new situations with confidence and a high tolerance for ambiguity

0	I	2	3	4	5

15. _____

0	I	2	3	4	5

AS A PROGRAM DEVELOPER

Understanding the Planning Process

1. Ability to describe and implement the basic steps—for example, climate setting, needs assessment, formulation of program objectives, program design, program execution, and evaluation—that undergird the planning process in adult education

0	I	2	3	4	5

2. Ability to involve representatives of client systems appropriately in the planning process

0	I	2	3	4	5

3. Ability to develop and use instruments and procedures for assessing the needs of individuals, organizations, and subpopulations in social systems

0	I	2	3	4	5

4. Ability to use strategies of systems analysis in program planning

0	I	2	3	4	5

5. _____   0   1   2   3   4   5
   _____

Designing and Operating Programs

1. Ability to construct a variety of program designs to   0   1   2   3   4   5
meet the needs of various situations—for example, basic
skills training, developmental education, management
development, and organizational development.

2. Ability to design programs with a creative variety of for-   0   1   2   3   4   5
mats, activities, schedules, resources, and evaluative proce-
dures

3. Ability to use needs assessments, census data, organiza-   0   1   2   3   4   5
tional records, surveys, and so forth in adapting programs to
specific needs and clientele

4. Ability to use planning mechanisms—such as advisory   0   1   2   3   4   5
councils, committees, and task forces—effectively

5. Ability to develop and carry out a plan for program   0   1   2   3   4   5
evaluation that will satisfy the requirements of institutional
accountability and provide for program improvement

6. _____   0   1   2   3   4   5
   _____

AS AN ADMINISTRATOR

Understanding Organizational Development and Maintenance

1. Ability to describe and apply theories and research   0   1   2   3   4   5
findings about organizational behavior, management, and
renewal

2. Ability to form a personal philosophy of administration   0   1   2   3   4   5
and to adapt it to various organizational situations

3. Ability to form policies that clearly convey the defini-   0   1   2   3   4   5
tion of an organization's mission, social philosophy, educa-
tional commitment, and so forth

4. Ability to evaluate organizational effectiveness and to   0   1   2   3   4   5
guide its continuous self-renewal processes

5. Ability to plan effectively with and through others, shar-   0   1   2   3   4   5
ing responsibilities and decision making with them as
appropriate

6. Ability to select, supervise, and provide for in-service   0   1   2   3   4   5
education of personnel

7. Ability to evaluate staff performance

0	I	2	3	4	5

8. Ability to analyze and interpret legislation affecting adult education

0	I	2	3	4	5

9. Ability to describe financial policies and practices in the field of adult education and to use them as guidelines for setting your own policies and practices

0	I	2	3	4	5

10. Ability to perform the role of change agent vis-à-vis organizations and communities using educational processes

0	I	2	3	4	5

11. _____

0	I	2	3	4	5

Understanding Program Administration

1. Ability to design and operate programs within a limited budget

0	I	2	3	4	5

2. Ability to make and monitor financial plans and procedures

0	I	2	3	4	5

3. Ability to convey convincingly to policymakers modern approaches to adult education and training

0	I	2	3	4	5

4. Ability to design and use promotion, publicity, and public relations strategies appropriately and effectively

0	I	2	3	4	5

5. Ability to prepare grant proposals and identify potential funding sources for them

0	I	2	3	4	5

6. Ability to use consultants' expertise appropriately

0	I	2	3	4	5

7. Ability and willingness to experiment with programmatic innovations and to assess their results objectively

0	I	2	3	4	5

8. _____

0	I	2	3	4	5

9. _____

0	I	2	3	4	5

10. _____

0	I	2	3	4	5

Figure 2. Competency Diagnostic and Planning Guide

	Importance to my career or self-actualization				Level of present development				Level of priority			
	None	Low	Med.	High	None	Low	Med.	High	None	Low	Med.	High
UNIT I. DESIGNING LEARNING EXPERIENCES												
Characteristics of Adult Learners												
Ability to describe and apply modern concepts and research findings about the needs, interests, motivations, capacities, and developmental characteristics of adults as learners												
Ability to describe the differences between youths and adults as learners and the implications of these differences for teaching and learning												
Ability to assess the effects on learning of forces from the larger environment—for example, from groups, organizations, and communities												
The Process of Designing Learning Experiences												
Ability to describe the difference between a content plan and a process design												
Ability to design learning experiences for a variety of purposes that take into account individual differences among learners												

	Importance to my career or self-actualization				Level of present development				Level of priority			
	None	Low	Med.	High	None	Low	Med.	High	None	Low	Med.	High
Role of the Teacher												
Ability to conceptualize and explain the role of the teacher as a facilitator and resource to self-directed learners												
Ability to engineer a physical and psychological climate of mutual respect, trust, collaboration, openness, support, and safety												
Ability to establish a warm, empathic, facilitative relationship with learners of all sorts												
Ability to engage learners responsibly in self-diagnoses of needs for learning												
Ability to engage learners in formulating goals, objectives, and directions of growth in terms that are meaningful to them												
Ability to involve learners in the planning, conducting, and evaluating of learning activities appropriately												
Helping Learners Become Self-Directing												
Ability to explain the conceptual differences between didactic instruction and self-directed learning												

	Importance to my career or self-actualization				Level of present development				Level of priority			
	None	Low	Med.	High	None	Low	Med.	High	None	Low	Med.	High
Ability to design and conduct one-hour, three-hour, one-day, and three-day learning experiences to develop the skills for self-directed learning												
Ability to model the role of a self-directed learner in your own behavior												
UNIT 2. SELECTING METHODS, TECHNIQUES, AND MATERIALS												
Methods, Techniques, and Materials												
Ability to describe the range of methods or formats for organizing learning experiences												
Ability to describe the range of techniques available for facilitating learning												
Ability to describe the range of materials available as resources for learning												
Methods and Techniques for Achieving Learning Objectives												
Ability to describe various theories of learning and their implications for the selection of methods, techniques, and materials												

	Importance to my career or self-actualization				Level of present development				Level of priority			
	None	Low	Med.	High	None	Low	Med.	High	None	Low	Med.	High
Ability to provide a rationale for selecting a particular method, technique, or material for achieving a particular educational objective												
Ability to evaluate the effectiveness of various methods, techniques, and materials in achieving particular educational outcomes												
UNIT 3. SKILL IN A SPECTRUM OF TECHNIQUES												
Climate-Setting Techniques												
Ability to present yourself as a genuine human being, not just someone performing the role of teacher												
Ability to use several techniques for helping learners become acquainted with one another												
Ability to use several techniques to help learners identify their resources												
Ability to conduct several skill-practice exercises in self-directed learning												
Diagnostic Techniques												
Ability to develop and manage procedures for constructing competency models												

	Importance to my career or self-actualization				Level of present development				Level of priority			
	None	Low	Med.	High	None	Low	Med.	High	None	Low	Med.	High
Ability to develop and manage procedures for constructing performance-assessment tools and procedures												
Ability to conduct diagnostic interviews												
Ability to administer achievement tests, aptitude tests, and other standardized diagnostic tests												
Presentation Techniques												
Ability to present information, provide inspiration, and stimulate inquiry through speaking												
Ability to use television and videotape programs appropriately												
Ability to use a variety of platform techniques, including debate, dialogue, group interview, symposium, panel discussion, demonstration, and colloquy												
Ability to use audiocassette programs appropriately												
Ability to use programmed instruction appropriately												
Ability to select or construct multimedia package programs appropriately												

	Importance to my career or self-actualization				Level of present development				Level of priority			
	None	Low	Med.	High	None	Low	Med.	High	None	Low	Med.	High
Ability to use motion pictures, film strips, and slides appropriately												
Ability to use dramatization techniques appropriately												
Ability to use recordings appropriately												
Ability to use exhibits as a resource for learning												
Ability to use trips as a resource for learning												
Audience-Participation Techniques for Large Meetings												
Ability to use question-and-answer periods effectively												
Ability to use the forum technique												
Ability to use listening teams												
Ability to use reaction panels												
Ability to use buzz groups												
Ability to use audience role plays												
Discussion and Counseling Techniques												
Ability to lead guided discussions												

	Importance to my career or self-actualization				Level of present development				Level of priority			
	None	Low	Med.	High	None	Low	Med.	High	None	Low	Med.	High
Ability to use book-based discussions												
Ability to lead Socratic discussions												
Ability to lead problem-solving discussions												
Ability to lead case discussions												
Ability to lead group-centered discussions												
Ability to use coaching and counseling techniques												
Simulation Techniques												
Ability to use role plays												
Ability to use the critical-incident process												
Ability to use the case method												
Ability to use simulation and skill-practice exercises												
Ability to use gaming techniques												
Ability to use participative cases												

	Importance to my career or self-actualization				Level of present development				Level of priority			
	None	Low	Med.	High	None	Low	Med.	High	None	Low	Med.	High
Group Process Techniques												
Ability to use human relations laboratory and sensitivity training techniques												
Ability to use transactional analysis												
Ability to use gestalt techniques												
Audiovisual and Other Resource Materials												
Ability to construct and use a variety of audio-visual materials												
Ability to construct study guides, workbooks, and other teacher-made materials												
Ability to develop programmed learning and computer-managed instructional materials												
Evaluation Techniques												
Ability to evaluate learning procedures and outcomes and to select or construct appropriate instruments for this purpose												
Ability to assess performance before and after a learning experience to measure effects												

❖ Exhibit 2-2. Guidelines for Using Learning Contracts ❖

One of the most significant findings from adult-learning research—such as Tough's *The Adult's Learning Projects* (Ontario Institute for Studies in Education, 1979)—is that, when adults learn something naturally rather than "being taught," they are highly self-directing. Evidence is also accumulating that shows that what adults learn on their own initiative they learn more keenly and permanently than what they learn by being "taught."

Learning that is done for personal development can probably be planned and carried out completely by individuals on their own terms. But those kinds of learning that need to improve professional competence must take into account the needs and expectations of organizations, professions, and society. Learning contracts provide a means for negotiating a reconciliation between external needs and expectations and the learner's internal needs and interests.

Furthermore, in traditional education the learning activity is structured by the teacher and the institution. The learners are told what objectives to work toward, what resources they are to use, how to use these resources, and how accomplishing the objectives will be evaluated. This imposed structure conflicts with the adult's deep psychological need to be self-directing and may induce resistance, apathy, or withdrawal. Learning contracts provide a vehicle for making the planning of learning experiences a mutual undertaking between learners and their helpers, mentors, and peers. By participating in the process of diagnosing their learning needs, forming objectives, identifying resources, choosing learning strategies, and evaluating accomplishments, the learners develop a sense of ownership and commitment to the learning plan.

Finally, in supervised field experiences, what work is to be done will be clearer to both the learner and field supervisor than what is to be learned from the experience. There is a long tradition of field-experience learners being exploited for the performance of menial tasks that the paid workers don't want to do. The learning contract is a way to make the learning objectives of the field experience clear and explicit for both the learner and the field supervisor.

How Do You Develop a Learning Contract?

Step 1: Diagnose Your Learning Needs

A learning need is the gap between where you are now and where you want to be in a particular set of competencies. You may already be aware of certain learning needs as a result of a personnel appraisal process or your own accumulation of evidence of the gaps between where you are now and where you would like to be. If not, it might be worthwhile to go through this process.

First, construct a model of the competencies required to perform a role you are concerned about, such as parent, teacher, civic leader, manager, consumer, or professional worker. A competency model that you can use as a thought-starter and checklist may already exist. If not, you can build your own model with the help of friends, colleagues, supervisors, and resource people.

Think of a competency as the ability to do something at some level of proficiency. It usually comprises knowledge, understanding, skills, attitudes, and values. For example, the ability to ride a bicycle from my home to the store is a competency that involves some knowledge of how a bicycle operates and the route to the store; an understanding of some of the dangers inherent in riding a bicycle; skill in mounting, pedaling, steering, and stopping a bicycle; an attitude of desire to ride the bicycle; and a valuing of the exercise it will yield. The ability to ride a bicycle in a cross-country race would be a higher-level competency that would require greater knowledge, understanding, and skill. Producing a competency model, even if it is crude and subjective, will provide a clear sense of direction.

Having constructed a competency model, your next task is to assess the gap between where you are now and where the model says you should be with regard to each competency. You can do this alone or with the help of people who have been observing your performance. Chances are you will find that you have already developed some competencies, and you can concentrate on those you haven't yet developed.

Step 2: Specify Your Learning Objectives

You are now ready to start filling out the first column of the learning contract in Figure 3, labeled "Learning Objectives." Each of the learning needs diagnosed in Step 1 should be translated into a learning objective. Be sure your objectives describe what you will learn, not what you will do to learn them. For example, "to read five books" is not a learning objective, but a strategy for using resources. The learning objective would describe what you want to learn by reading five books. State your objectives in whatever terms are most meaningful to you: content acquisition, terminal behaviors, or directions of growth.

Step 3: Specify Learning Resources and Strategies

When you have finished listing your objectives, move to the second column of the contract, "Learning Resources and Strategies," and describe how you propose to go about accomplishing each objective. Identify the material and human resources you plan to use and the strategies (i.e., techniques and tools) you will use in making use of them. Also at this stage, decide when you will have learned the objectives. See Figure 4, "Example Learning Contract."

Step 4: Specify Evidence of Accomplishment

Move to the fourth column, "Evidence of Accomplishment of Objectives," and describe what evidence you will collect to indicate the degree to which you have achieved each objective. Perhaps the examples in Figure 5, "Example Evidence of Objective Accomplishment," will stimulate your thinking about what evidence you might accumulate.

Step 5: Specify How the Evidence Will Be Validated

After you have specified what evidence you will collect for each objective in column four, move to the fifth column, "Criteria and Means for Validating Evidence." For each objective, first specify the criteria by which the evidence is to be judged. The criteria will vary according to the type of objective. For example, criteria for knowledge objectives might include depth, comprehensiveness, precision, clarity, accuracy, usefulness, and scholarliness. For skill objectives, the criteria might include poise, speed, precision, flexibility, gracefulness, style, and imagination. For attitudes and values, they might include consistency, immediacy of action, or confidence in action.

After you have specified the criteria, indicate how you propose to have the evidence judged according to these criteria. For example, if you produce a paper or report as evidence of accomplishment of a knowledge objective, who will read it and what are their qualifications? Will they express their judgments by rating scales, descriptive reports, or evaluative reports? If you are getting a rating of how well you accomplished a skill objective, who will observe you performing the skill—students, peers, or experts? What kind of feedback about your performance will you ask them to give you? One of the actions that helps to differentiate distinguished performance from adequate performance in self-directed learning is the wisdom with which learners select their validators.

Step 6: Review Your Contract With Consultants

After you have completed the first draft of your contract, you will find it useful to review it with two or three friends, supervisors, or other consultants to get their reactions and suggestions. Here are some questions you might ask them:

- Are the learning objectives clear, understandable, and realistic? Do they describe accurately what I propose to learn?
- Can you think of other objectives I might consider?
- Do the learning strategies and resources seem reasonable, appropriate, and efficient? Can you suggest other resources?
- Does the evidence seem relevant to the various objectives, and would it convince you? Can you think of other evidence I might consider?
- Are the criteria and means for validating the evidence clear, relevant, and convincing? Can you think of other evidence that I might consider?

Exhibit 2-3, "Consultation Exercise," will facilitate this review process.

Step 7: Carry Out the Contract

You now simply do what the contract calls for. But keep in mind that, as you work on it, you may find that your notions about what you want to learn and how you want to learn it may change. Therefore, don't hesitate to revise your contract as you go.

Step 8: Evaluate Your Learning

When you have completed your contract, you will want to get some assurance that you have in fact learned what you set out to learn. Perhaps the simplest way to do this is to ask the consultants you used in Step 6 to examine your evidence and validation data and give you their judgment about the data's adequacy.

Figure 3. A Learning Contract

Learner _____   Learning experience _____

Learning Objectives	Learning Resources and Strategies	Completion Date	Evidence of Accomplishment of Objectives	Criteria and Means for Validating Evidence
What are you going to learn?	How are you going to learn it?	What is your target date for completion?	How are you going to know that you learned it?	How are you going to prove that you learned it?

Figure 4. Example Learning Contract

Learner _____ Learning experience _____

Learning Objectives	Learning Resources and Strategies	Completion Date	Evidence of Accomplishment of Objectives	Criteria and Means for Validating Evidence
To improve my ability to organize my work efficiently so I can accomplish 20 percent more work in a day.	1. Find and read books and articles in the library on how to organize work and manage time. 2. Interview three executives on how they organize their work, then observe them for one day each, noting techniques they use. 3. Select the best techniques from each and plan a day's work.	In three weeks.	Have a colleague observe me for a day, giving me feedback.	1. The amount of work I do each day increases by 20 percent. 2. A colleague who knows my former work output will measure my new work output and will give me the percentage increase I've made.

Figure 5. Example Evidence of Objective Accomplishment

TYPE OF OBJECTIVE	EXAMPLES OF EVIDENCE
Knowledge	Reports of knowledge acquired—in essays, examinations, oral presentations, audiovisual presentations, and annotated bibliographies
Understanding	Examples of using knowledge to solve problems—in action projects, research projects with conclusions and recommendations, program planning, and organizational change proposals
Skills	Performance exercises, simulations, demonstrations, use of videotapes of performance, and so on
Attitudes	Attitudinal rating scales, role playing, simulation exercises, critical incident cases, diaries, and so on
Values	Value rating scales, performance in values clarification groups, critical incident cases, simulation exercises, and so on

❖ Exhibit 2-3. Consultation Exercise ❖

I introduce this exercise by explaining that its purpose is to provide an opportunity for learners to sharpen their skills in giving and receiving help in the consultation process. I ask the learners to form groups of three. If the group isn't divisible by three, I invite the one or two left over to serve as roving observers.

I then ask each member of each group to take a letter (*A*, *B*, or *C*), and I explain that there will be three rounds of about 20 minutes each. In Round 1, *A* will be the consultant, *B* the client, and *C* the observer. In Round 2, *B* will be the consultant, *C* the client, and *A* the observer. In Round 3, *C* will be the consultant, *A* the client, and *B* the observer.

I then ask them to look at the "Observer's Guide Sheet" that they were given when they entered the room (see Figure 6), while I explain its use. I tell them that the behaviors on the left side of the sheet are those of the old-fashioned type of consultants, who saw it as their responsibility to solve problems for their clients. The behaviors on the right side of the sheet are those of modern consultants, who see it as their responsibility to help their clients solve their own problems. I tell the observer to watch what the consultant does and to note any statement made by the consultant in the block the observer thinks appropriate. This way the observer can report it in language as similar to the consultant's as possible.

I ask the first round to proceed, using 15 minutes for the consultation and five minutes for the observer's report, then continue with Round 2 and Round 3.

At the end of the three rounds, I invite the learners to share with the whole group what they found most and least helpful about what their consultants did, and to raise any questions about the consultation process that they want me to respond to.

Figure 6. Observer's Guide Sheet

Note the instances in which the person you are observing in the helping role—

Suggests problems, facts, solutions, actions, and so forth	**Versus**	**Asks** the client for clarification of the client's perceptions, facts, solutions, and so forth
Interprets the client's feelings, motivations, inadequacies, and so forth	**Versus**	**Seeks to understand** the client's feelings, ideas, motivations, and so forth
Conveys doubts about the client's ability to cope with difficulty	**Versus**	**Encourages and supports** the client in using the client's own abilities

❖ Exhibit 2-4. Suggestions for Inquiry Teams ❖

Your productivity as a group will depend to a large extent on building cohesive relationships in the beginning. It will pay dividends later if you will take some time at your first meeting to find out who you all are as role performers and as human beings. One way to accomplish this is to share with one another your work experience, career aspirations, interests in life, reasons for taking this course, special resources you bring into this course that might be useful to others, your feelings as you enter into this experience, and anything else that will help your colleagues see you as a unique human being.

As your group gets to work, there may be times when the group seems to be bogged down or not working well together. On such occasions it may be helpful to suggest that group members fill out the "Process Rating Sheet for Inquiry Teams" in Figure 7. Then, with a show of hands, find out how many are at the low or high ends of each scale. This will identify problems that can be discussed and solved.

If any members of the team feel they just can't accomplish what they want to through the group, they should feel free to move to another group or to pursue their contract objectives through independent study.

Organizing for Work

The first task, after relationships have been established, is to be sure that the group is clear about its goals. Each team has the responsibility of planning and conducting a learning experience for the rest of the class involving one of the inquiry units listed in the course's syllabus.

You now need to take these (or equivalent) steps to decide what you will do with this unit:

▪ Decide how you will find out what your classmates want to learn about this unit—for example, through questionnaires or interviews.

▪ Using this information, decide what the objectives of the learning experience in this unit will be.

Now, having decided on what you want to help your classmates learn about your unit, you need to design the learning experience. Some general guidelines for doing this are suggested in Knowles's *The Modern Practice of Adult Education: From Pedagogy to Andragogy* (Follett Press, 1980), pp. 288-297. Here are two key questions you might ask yourself as you plan the design:

▪ Are you making adequate provisions in the design for the active participation of your classmates?

▶ Are they learning by doing as well as by listening?

Then you need to decide how you will have your learning experience and your performance evaluated.

Finally, you need to agree on which members of your team will take responsibility for each element in the planning, conducting, and evaluating of your learning experience.

A final suggestion: This is one of the few times you will have an opportunity to try new things with minimal consequences for mistakes, so be adventuresome!

Figure 7. Process Rating Sheet for Inquiry Teams

Circle one number in each scale. Do not sign your name on this form.

	Low				High
	1	2	3	4	5
1. What is the degree of your feeling of satisfaction with this team?	1	2	3	4	5
2. How clear is the team about its goals and tasks?	1	2	3	4	5
3. How well are team members listening to one another?	1	2	3	4	5
4. To what extent did you contribute to the work of the team today?	1	2	3	4	5
5. To what extent were your ideas accepted and used by the team?	1	2	3	4	5
6. To what extent did one or two team members dominate the discussion?	1	2	3	4	5
7. To what extent did you personally resent overparticipation by other members?	1	2	3	4	5
8. To what extent did team members prepare themselves—for example, by doing background reading—for this meeting?	1	2	3	4	5
9. How well is the team organizing itself for its work?	1	2	3	4	5
10. To what extent do you think the team should make better use of outside resources?	1	2	3	4	5
11. To what extent does the team recognize its problems and conflicts, and deal with them openly?	1	2	3	4	5

12. What suggestions would you like to make to improve the team's operation?

_____
_____
_____
_____
_____
_____

CHAPTER 3

Designs for Courses

This chapter presents the designs of several courses I have facilitated. Although all of these courses had adult education as their content area, many of my colleagues and former students have adapted these designs to such other subject areas as liberal arts, nursing, medicine, accounting, and business management.

The exhibits open with a comparison of two designs of the same course taught at different times. Exhibit 3-1, "The Nature of Adult Education," was offered at Boston University from 1960 to 1974, in classes of 30 students. It operated like a seminar, with small groups interacting with the whole class. Exhibit 3-2, "Adult Education: History, Philosophy, and Contemporary Nature," was offered at North Carolina State University from 1974 to 1979, with 50 to 75 students in each class. It used inquiry teams and learning contracts. My role in both was as a process manager and a content resource.

Exhibit 3-3, "Adult Learning Concepts and Theories," is a course I have conducted at several universities, sometimes under the title, "The Adult Learner."

Exhibit 3-4, "Program Planning and Methodology in Adult Education," is another course I have conducted at several universities under such alternate titles as "The Modern Practice of Adult Education" and "Adult Education Methods."

Exhibit 3-5, "Facilitating Self-Directed Learning" is a course I have conducted at the Oklahoma State University and the University of South Florida.

Exhibit 3-6, "Training and the Applied Behavioral Sciences," is a course I have conducted only once, at the University of Southern California's Washington Public Affairs Center.

In this chapter:

❖ Exhibit 3-1. The Nature of Adult Education ❖

Objectives
The general objectives of this course, subject to modification by the individual objectives of the student, are to develop or strengthen the following competencies:
> an appreciation of the role of adult education in society, past and present, and exploration of its potential roles in the future
> knowledge of the present scope and trends of adult education in terms of aims, agencies, content, personnel, program types, methods and materials, and problems and obstacles
> an understanding of the concerns and philosophical issues affecting the adult educational field
> insight into the relationship between the education of adults and the education of youths
> an understanding of the basic process of adult education.

Students who want credit in this course will be evaluated on the basis of criteria and procedures determined mutually by the instructor and the students.

Resources
The following books are basic references for the course:

Houle, Cyril O. *The Design of Education.* Jossey-Bass Publishers, 1972a.

Knowles, Malcolm S. *The Adult Education Movement in the United States.* Holt, Rinehart & Winston, 1962.

—. *The Modern Practice of Adult Education: From Pedagogy to Andragogy.* Follett Press, 1980.

Smith, Robert M., George F. Aker, and J.R. Kidd. *Handbook of Adult Education.* Macmillan Publishing Co., 1970.

Other books that have resources relevant to the particular inquiry units are identified in the section titled "Process Design." When page numbers are not specified for a given reference, it is suggested that the learners look up relevant information in the reference's table of contents and index. Full reference listings are in the master bibliography at the end of this book.

Process Design

I.   **Orientation**

    A. Introduction of group members, with description of roles in adult education

    B. Assessment of learners' present knowledge, understanding, and perceptions of the adult educational field (in small groups)

    C. Formulation of objectives of the course: analysis of instructor's objectives and modification by students' objectives (in small groups)

    D. Organization of the course plan: sequence of inquiry, division of responsibility, plan for evaluation

II. **The role of adult education in society**

    A. Historical role

        —Knowles (1960), pp. 7-28.
        —Grattan (1955), pp. 3-17, 135-286.
        —Knowles (1962), pp. 3-154.
        —Houle (1972a), pp. 2-30, 237-241.
        —Smith, et al. (1970), pp. xvii-xxx.

    B. Contemporary needs

        —Knowles (1960), pp. 3-6, 29-38.
        —Knowles (1980), chapters 1-2.
        —Sheats, et al. (1953), pp. 15-67.
        —Knowles (1950), pp. 3-10.
        —Verner (1964), pp. 3-7.
        —Kempfer (1955), pp. 17-58.
        —Smith, et al. (1970), pp. 3-23.

C. Aims of adult education as a movement

　—Powell (1956), pp. 12-30.
　—Sheats, et al. (1953), pp. 2-14.
　—A Design for Democracy (1956), pp. 51-55, 59-77.
　—Knowles (1960), pp. 151-155.
　—Verner (1964), pp. 7-10.
　—Kempfer (1955), pp. 3-16.
　—Smith, et al. (1970), pp. 25-44.
　—Houle (1972a), pp. 250-256.

III. Scope of adult education

A. Agencies of adult education in the United States

1. Types of agencies

　—Brunner, et al. (1959), pp. 211-228.
　—Powell (1956), pp. 33-61.
　—Knowles (1962), pp. 157-188.
　—Johnstone and Rivera (1965), chapter 2.
　—Smith, et al. (1970), pp. 171-190.

a) Those primarily for the education of youth

(1) Public schools

　—Knowles (1960), pp. 345-355.
　—Sheats, et al. (1953), pp. 144-174.
　—Grattan (1955), pp. 217-231.
　—Knowles (1962), pp. 24-30, 52-60, 133-145.
　—Smith, et al. (1970), pp. 231-244.

(2) Colleges and universities

　—Knowles (1960), pp. 203, 217.
　—Sheats, et al. (1953), pp. 175-199.
　—Grattan (1955), pp. 183-196.
　—Knowles (1962), pp. 46-50, 83-90.
　—Smith, et al. (1970), pp. 191-230.

b) Those which are primarily adult educational

(1) Agricultural extension

—Knowles (1960), pp. 218-229.
—Sheats, et al. (1953), pp. 98-119.
—Grattan (1955), pp. 197-216.
—Knowles (1960), pp. 90-94, 163-164.
—Smith, et al. (1970), pp. 265-282.

(2) Independent centers

—Knowles (1960), pp. 263-273.
—Knowles (1962), pp. 105-107.
—Smith, et al. (1970), pp. 389-391.

(3) Proprietary schools

—Knowles (1960), pp. 339-344.
—Knowles (1962), pp. 131-133.
—Smith, et al. (1970), pp. 387-389.

c) Those that have adult education as a coordinate function

(1) Libraries

—Knowles (1962), 302-313.
—Sheats, et al. (1953), pp. 120-143.
—Grattan (1955), pp. 232-238.
—Knowles (1962), 7-8, 19-20, 51-52, 112-118.
—Smith, et al. (1970), pp. 245-252.

(2) Museums

—Knowles (1960), pp. 330-338.
—Knowles (1962), pp. 20, 74, 130-131.
—Smith, et al. (1970), pp. 252-260.

(3) Social welfare and health agencies

—Knowles (1960), pp. 336-377, 255-262.
—Knowles (1962), pp. 64-65, 103-105, 164-165.
—Smith, et al. (1970), pp. 252-260.

d) Those in which adult education is a supporting function

(1) Business and industry

—Knowles (1960), pp. 196-202.
—Knowles (1962), pp. 79-83.
—Smith, et al. (1970), pp. 315-334.

(2) Foundations

—Knowles (1960), pp. 196-202.
—Knowles (1962), pp. 94-97, 190-194, 241-242.

(3) Government agencies

—Knowles (1960), pp. 238-254.
—Knowles (1962), pp. 97-103, 136-137.
—Smith, et al. (1970), pp. 285-300.

(4) International organizations

—Knowles (1960), pp. 274-285.
—Sheats, et al. (1953), pp. 273-292.
—Smith, et al. (1970), pp. 45-58.

(5) Labor unions

—Knowles (1960), pp. 286-301.
—Sheats, et al. (1953), pp. 221-245.
—Grattan (1955), pp. 239-256.
—Knowles (1962), pp. 44-45, 107-111.
—Smith, et al. (1970), pp. 301-314.

(6) Mass media

    —Knowles (1960), pp. 314-329.
    —Knowles (1962), pp. 109-110, 118-130.
    —Smith, et al. (1970), pp. 96-102.

(7) Religious institutions

    —Knowles (1960), pp. 356-365.
    —Knowles (1962), pp. 9, 22-23, 72-73, 145-151.
    —Smith, et al. (1970), pp. 353-370.

(8) Voluntary associations

    —Knowles (1960), pp. 378-390.
    —Sheats, et al. (1953), pp. 200-220.
    —Grattan (1955), pp. 257-275.
    —Knowles (1962), pp. 21-22, 60-72, 151-154.
    —Smith, et al. (1970), pp. 172-180.

B. Content areas of adult education

—Knowles (1960), pp. 393-550.
—Powell (1956), pp. 97-181.
—Knowles (1962), pp. 255-256.
—Johnstone and Rivera (1965), chapter 2.
—Smith, et al. (1970), pp. 397-526.

C. Personnel of adult education

1. Leadership

    —Kempfer (1955), pp. 228-314.
    —Knowles (1960), pp. 117-128.
    —Brunner (1959), pp. 177-190.
    —Sheats, et al. (1953), pp. 399-426.
    —Powell (1956), pp. 199-219.
    —Knowles (1962), pp. 253-254.
    —Verner (1964), pp. 34-49.
    —Smith, et al. (1970), pp. 109-120.

—Houle (1972a), pp. 155-158, 290-292.

2. Clientele

—Brunner (1959), pp. 89-118.
—Johnstone and Rivera (1965), chapters 3-4.
—Verner (1964), pp. 18-33.

D. Program development

—Brunner (1959), pp. 125-141.
—Houle (1972a), pp. 31-225, 243-247.
—Kempfer (1955), pp. 61-290.
—Knowles (1960), pp. 65-81.
—Knowles (1980), chapter 9.
—Knowles (1950), pp. 84-166.
—Sheats, et al. (1953), pp. 68-81.
—Smith, et al. (1970), pp. 59-74.
—Verner (1964), pp. 50-67.

E. Methods of adult education

—Knowles (1960), pp. 82-95.
—Knowles (1980), chapter 11.
—Brunner (1959), pp. 142-176.
—Sheats, et al. (1953), pp. 321-348.
—Johnstone and Rivera (1965), chapter 2.
—Verner (1964) p. 68.
—Smith, et al. (1970), pp. 91-108.
—Houle (1972a), pp. 90-130, 274-285, 292-293.

F. Materials of adult education

—Knowles (1960), pp. 96-105.
—Sheats, et al. (1953), pp. 349-379.
—Smith, et al. (1970), pp. 75-90.
—Houle (1972a), pp. 152-155, 289-290.

IV. Problems and concerns in adult education

A. Coordination and role clarification

—Knowles (1960), pp. 179-195.
—Brunner (1959), pp. 211-242.
—Sheats, et al. (1953), pp. 246-272, 294-320.
—Knowles (1962), pp. 190-268.
—Kempfer (1955), pp. 293-313.
—Smith, et al. (1970), pp. 178-180.

B. Research and evaluation

—Kempfer (1955), pp. 399-421.
—Knowles (1960), pp. 106-116, 162-175.
—Brunner (1959), pp. 1-7, 243-273.
—Sheats, et al. (1953), pp. 448-474.
—Verner (1964), pp. 91-105.
—Smith, et al. (1970), pp. 70-74, 137-150.
—Houle (1972a), pp. 169-171, 182-184, 295-295, 299-300.

C. Public understanding

—Knowles (1960), pp. 129-137.
—Sheats, et al. (1953), pp. 448-474.
—Kempfer (1955), pp. 339-362.

D. Finance

—Knowles (1960), pp. 138-151.
—Sheats, et al. (1953), pp. 380-398.
—Powell (1956), pp. 220-227.
—Kempfer (1955), pp. 363-398.
—Houle (1972a), pp. 177-179, 298.

E. Facilities

—Knowles (1960), pp. 156-161.

F. Philosophical issues

—Knowles (1960), pp. 41-53.
—Powell (1956), pp. 231-235.
—Sillars (1958).
—Houle (1972a), pp. 241-143, 247-272.
—Smith, et al. (1970), pp. 121-136.

V. Adult education in other countries

VI. Trends and strategies for the future

—Knowles (1960), pp. 553-561.
—Sheats, et al. (1953), pp. 475-505.
—Powell (1956), pp. 185-198.
—Grattan (1955), pp. 303-310.
—Knowles (1962), pp. 269-280.
—Verner (1964), pp. 106-111.
—Houle (1972a), pp. 225.
—Smith, et al. (1970), pp. 151-167.

❖ Exhibit 3-2. Adult Education: History, Philosophy, and Contemporary Nature ❖

Objectives
The purpose of this course is provide resources for learners to develop or strengthen the following competencies:
- an understanding of adult education as a social movement and its role in society, including
  - —the historical evolution of adult education as a field of study and practice
  - —the optional values, aims, and assumptions that have guided and could guide adult education as an instrument of society
  - —the ways in which adult education has and has not influenced the development of American society
  - —the contemporary issues, problems, and needs in society, and adult education's responses to them
  - —potential future societal needs and what adult education's response to them should be
- knowledge of the scope and structure of adult education as a field of operations, including
  - —a panorama of institutions serving the educational needs of adults and their respective objectives, clientele, programs, and strategies
  - —the functions, positions, and roles performed by adult educators and conditions, standards, and bases of compensation for these roles
  - —the pre-service and in-service opportunities in professional education for the role of adult educator
  - —the mechanisms created for professional association among people, interagency planning, and coordination of resources in the field
  - —the learning projects adults do outside institutional auspices
  - —the relationship of adult education in this country to the education of adults around the world
- knowledge of adult education as a discipline and field of study, including
  - —the conceptual foundations—including theories about learning, adult development, organizational dynamics, and program development—that undergird adult educational operations
  - —the field's financial policies and practices

—the effects of physical environments on adult learning and how these have affected physical facilities in the field

—the major areas of past research investigations in the field of adult education and their designs, methods, and findings

—the methods, techniques, and materials used in the field.

Resources

Basic References

The following references will serve as the basic material resources for this course:

Knowles, Malcolm S. *Self-Directed Learning: A Guide for Learners and Teachers.* Follett Press, 1975.

—. *The Adult Education Movement in the United States,* revised edition. Krieger Publishing Co., 1977.

Smith, Robert M., George F. Aker, and J.R. Kidd. *Handbook of Adult Education.* Macmillan Publishing Co., 1970.

Additional lists of books that have resources relevant to the particular inquiry units are identified in the section titled "Inquiry Units" beginning on page 51. When page numbers are not specified for a given reference, it is suggested that the learners look up relevant information in the reference's table of contents and index. Full reference listings are in the master bibliography at the end of this book.

Periodical References

Information relevant to many of the inquiry units will be found in the following periodicals:

Adult Education, the quarterly professional journal of the Adult Education Association of the United States.

Adult Leadership, the monthly practitioner's magazine of the Adult Education Association of the United States.

Community College Review, the quarterly journal of the Department of Adult and Community College Education, North Carolina State University.

Community and Junior College Journal, the monthly magazine of the American Association of Community and Junior Colleges.

Convergence, the quarterly journal of the International Council for Adult Education.

Journal of Extension, the bimonthly journal of the Cooperative Extension Service.

Human Resources

The members of the faculty of departments of adult and community college education will have special resources that are relevant to various inquiry units.

Proposed Plan of Inquiry

This course's plan of inquiry is as follows:

- Group members introduce themselves, identifying roles, backgrounds, interests, and resources.
- The facilitator sets a climate of mutuality, support, informality, warmth, openness, trust, and so forth. (See Exhibit 2-1, "Basic Climate-Setting Exercise.")
- The facilitator shares his or her philosophical and theoretical framework, perception of role, resources, and so forth.
- The facilitator reviews (and modifies with the learners) the purpose, objectives, and plan of work for this course.
- The facilitator reviews (and modifies with the learners) the proposed inquiry units, with learners making a preliminary assessment of competency-development needs. (See Figure 1, "Self-Diagnostic Rating Scale.")
- The facilitator reviews material and human resources for this inquiry.
- Learners self-diagnose learning needs.
- Learners draft learning contracts with the help of consultation triads, then negotiate with the facilitator. (See Exhibit 2-2, "Guidelines for Using Learning Contracts," and Exhibit 2-3, "Consultation Exercise.")
- Learners organize inquiry teams.
- Learners create learning experiences:
  —Each learner will have some objectives that can be accomplished best through independent study, field projects, or tutoring. Other

objectives can best be accomplished through involvement in an inquiry team. Still other objectives can best be accomplished through participation in the presentations of other inquiry teams.

—Each inquiry team will have the responsibility for mastering the content of its inquiry unit and designing and executing a learning experience for the rest of the class. During the inquiry team's planning, the facilitator will be available as a consultant and resource person.

—Each inquiry team will plan the schedule of its learning experience for the rest of the class so the facilitator will have at least half an hour for input and analysis of the experience.

Inquiry Units
I.   Unit 1

A. What are the characteristics of adult education as a social movement, and what has been its role in society?

1. How did it evolve historically as a field of study and social practice?

—Smith, et al. (1970), pp. xvii-xxiii, 25-43.
—Knowles (1980), pp. 7-38.
—Knowles (1962), pp. 3-154.
—Axford (1969), pp. 27-56.
—Brunner (1959).
—Grattan (1951).
—Grattan (1955).

2. What are the social philosophies that have guided and could guide adult education as an instrument of society (i.e, its values, aims, and so on)?

—Smith, et al. (1970), pp. 121-135.
—Knowles (1960), pp. 41-53.
—Bergevin (1967), pp. 7-40, 65-110.
—Lindeman (1956).
—Freire (1970).
—Lindeman (1926).

3. In what ways has adult education influenced or not influenced the development of American society?

—Knowles (1960), pp. 5-25, 29-38.
—Also see the references in Sections I.A.1 and I.A.2.

4. What are the contemporary issues, problems, and needs in society, and what are adult education's responses to them?

—Smith, et al. (1970), pp. 3-23.
—Commission on Non-Traditional Study (1973).
—Houle (1972b).
—Blakely (1965).
—Blakely (1971).
—Charters (1971).
—Cook, et al. (1969).

5. What are potential future societal needs, and what should adult education's response to them be?

—Smith, et al. (1970), pp. 151-167.
—Knowles (1960), pp. 553-561.
—Knowles (1962), pp. 269-349.

II. Unit 2

A. What is the scope and structure of adult education as a field of operations?

1. What institutions serve the educational needs of adults and what are their objectives, clientele, programs, and strategies?

—Smith, et al. (1970), pp. 171-526.
—Knowles (1960), pp. 179-550.
—Knowles (1962), pp. 76-154.
—Johnstone and Rivera (1965).

2. What are the various functions, positions, and roles performed by adult educators and the conditions, standards, and bases of compensation for these roles?

—Nadler (1970), pp. 147-247.
—Knowles (1980), pp. 21-35.

3. What are the opportunities and characteristics of graduate programs and in-service training programs for the professional development for adult educators?

—Smith, et al. (1970), pp. 109-119.
—Knowles (1960), pp. 69-102, 117-128, 307-326.

4. What mechanisms have been established for professional association and coordination in the field of adult education?

—Smith, et al. (1970), pp. 171-189, 75-90, 527-547.
—Knowles (1960), pp. 179-185.
—Knowles (1962), pp. 157-268, 327-334.

5. What adult learning takes place outside institutional programs, and how is experiential learning assessed for academic credit?

—Smith, et al. (1970), pp. 513-527.
—Tough (1979).
—Johnstone and Rivera (1965).

6. What is the relationship between adult education in this country and the education of adults around the world?

—Smith, et al. (1970), pp. 45-57.
—Knowles (1960), pp. 274-285.

III. Unit 3

A. What are the characteristics of adult education as a discipline and field of study?

1. What are the conceptual foundations of the field, and how do these differ from the conceptual foundations of other elements of the national educational enterprise?

—Smith, et al. (1970), pp. 25-43, 59-74.
—Knowles (1960), pp. 3-6, 27-39, 54-64, 65-81, 105-305.
—Kidd (1973).
—Knowles (1980), pp. 37-55, 99-129.
—Knowles (1984b), pp. 27-59.

2. What are the financial policies and practices in the field?

—Knowles (1960), pp. 138-155.

3. What are the effects of the physical environment on learning and how have these affected physical facilities in the field?

—Knowles (1960), pp. 156-161.
—Alford, (1968).

4. What have been the major areas of research in adult education and what have been their designs, methods, and findings?

—Smith, et al. (1970), pp. 137-149, 549-563.
—Knowles (1960), pp. 106-116.
—Brunner (1959).

❖ Exhibit 3-3. Adult Learning Concepts and Theories ❖

Objectives
The purpose of this course is to help learners develop or strengthen the following competencies:
- ▶ knowledge of the current concepts and research findings about the needs, interests, motivations, capacities, and developmental characteristics of adults as learners
- ▶ an understanding of the differences between youths and adults as learners and of the implications of these differences for teaching and learning
- ▶ insight into the processes and condition of adult learning and into the forces that affect learning in the dynamics of personal, group, and organizational behavior
- ▶ knowledge of the various theories of learning, and construction of a personal theory of learning
- ▶ an appreciation of the role and resources of an individual person in carrying on a continuing program of self-development.

In addition, special objectives of individual learners in this course will be assessed and incorporated into the curriculum.

Resources
The following references serve as the basic references for this course:

Kidd, J.R. *How Adults Learn*. Follett Press, 1973.

Knowles, Malcolm S. *The Adult Learner: A Neglected Species*. Gulf Publishing Co., 1978 (3d edition published 1984b).

Additional lists of books that have resources relevant to the particular inquiry units are identified in the section titled "Inquiry Units" beginning on page 56. When page numbers are not specified for a given reference, it is suggested that the learners look up relevant information in the reference's table of contents and index. Full reference listings are in the master bibliography at the end of this book.

Handouts for this course include Figure 1, "Self-Diagnostic Rating Scale," and Exhibit 2-4, "Suggestions for Inquiry Teams."

Process Design

This course's plan of inquiry is as follows:

- climate setting; see Exhibit 2-1, "Basic Climate-Setting Exercise"
- diagnosis of learning needs; see Figure 1, "Self-Diagnostic Rating Scale"
- organization of inquiry teams; see Exhibit 2-4, "Suggestions for Inquiry Teams"
- scheduling of inquiry team meetings and reports
- reporting of inquiry teams
- closing question-and-issues session
- evaluation of this course.

Inquiry Units

I.   **Unit 1**

A. What are the characteristics of adult learners?

1. How do adults learn? What is learning versus growth, change, and maturation? How do adults learn differently than children and youths? What are adults' unique characteristics as learners?

—Kidd (1973), pp. 13-52.
—Knowles (1984b), pp. 43-59.

2. What is the student body of adult education? How is "adult" defined in terms of education? How many adults are participating? In what ways are they different from nonparticipants? What is the potential student body? What types of content do they study? Where? What reasons do they give for enrolling?

3. What motivates adults to learn? What are learning needs? How do they evolve? What are the developmental tasks and teachable moments of adult life?

—Kidd (1973), pp. 100-112, 124-146.

—Knowles (1984b), pp. 23, 29-31, 45-46, 62, 97, 112, 113.

II. Unit 2

A. How does learning take place?

1. What is theory? What are the theories of learning? What kinds of learning are there? What are the main theories about them? What are their implications for adult learning?

—Kidd (1973), pp. 147-192.
—Knowles (1984b), pp. 1-59.

2. How do group processes affect learning? What are the forces in groups that facilitate and inhibit learning? What kinds of learning are most appropriate for group or individual learning? Under what conditions is learning in groups optimized?

—Kidd (1973), pp. 209-215.

3. How does the larger environment affect learning? What forces are at work in institutions, communities, and society-at-large that facilitate or inhibit learning? What are the main theories about institutional and social change, and how do educational processes fit into them? How can institutions and communities be changed to become more conducive environments for learning? What is organizational development? What would an optimally educative environment be like?

—Kidd (1973), pp. 193-267.
—Knowles (1984b), pp. 99-129.

III. Unit 3

A. What are the implications of learning theory for adult education?

1. What are the implications for organizing learning experiences? How can learning experiences be organized best to satisfy the needs of adult learners, be in step with their developmental

tasks, be relevant to their life experiences, take into account their unique characteristics, and promote their self-actualization? How is adult learning best reinforced and transferred?

—Kidd (1973), pp. 268-291.
—Knowles (1984b), pp. 99-129.

2. What are the implications for the role of the teacher? In what ways do modern ideas about learning call for changes in the traditional definitions of the role of the teacher? What is effective teaching? What are the responsibilities and strategies for educators?

—Kidd (1973), pp. 292-309.
—Knowles (1984b), pp. 60-98.

3. What are the implications of the concept of lifelong education for the field of education? How differently would children and youths be taught if they were taught to be lifelong learners? How would the educational system be organized and operated? What would be the role of nontraditional study?

❖ Exhibit 3-4. Program Planning and Methodology in Adult Education ❖

Assumptions

This study guide is based on the assumption that learning is an internal process with the locus of control of that process residing in the learner, but that this process can be facilitated by outside helpers. It further assumes that there are certain conditions more conducive to learning than others, and that these superior conditions are produced by practices in the learning-teaching transaction that adhere to superior principles of teaching. These conditions and principles are described in Knowles's *The Modern Practice of Adult Education: From Pedagogy to Andragogy* (Follett Press, 1980), pp. 57-58.

This study guide is based on certain assumptions about adults as learners and the learning process. These assumptions have some implications for what you do and how you will use the facilitator, your peers, and the resource materials. First, it assumes that you as a learner

▶ have the self-concept of being an adult and the desire and capability of taking responsibility for planning and managing your own learning with help from fellow students, the facilitator, and other helpers. It further assumes that what you learn through your own initiative you will learn more effectively than what you learn through imposition by others.

▶ bring with you into this activity a rich background of experience that is a valuable resource both for your own learning and for the learning of fellow students. It further assumes that your experience is different from the experience of other members of the course, and that your combined experiences represent a rich pool of resources for one another's learning.

▶ are readiest to learn those things you perceive will help you perform more effectively in your life tasks and allow you to achieve a higher level of potential. It further assumes that the study guide and the facilitator have an obligation to help you see how the course can help you perform more effectively.

▶ are unique, along with every other member of the course, with your own styles and paces of learning, outside commitments and pressures, goals, and internal motivations. It also assumes that your learning plans and strategies must be highly individualized.

Objectives

The purpose of this course is to help learners develop or strengthen the following competencies:

▶ knowledge of the basic principles and methods of program development and an understanding of their application in a variety of settings

▶ skill in the basic functions of program management, such as policy formulation; selecting, training, and supervising leaders and teachers; promoting and interpreting programs; financing; working with boards and committees; and program evaluation

▶ an understanding of the broad range of methods and techniques available to help adults learn, and skill in using these methods and techniques

▶ knowledge of the rationale for selecting particular methods and techniques for achieving particular educational objectives

▶ skill in designing learning experiences that use combinations of methods and techniques for optimal learning

▶ insight into the nature and dynamics of organizational life, and an understanding of the implications of these dynamics for the management of an adult educational enterprise

▶ an understanding of the role of the adult educator as a consultant and skill in using the consultation process to facilitate personal, group, and organizational change.

Resources

Books that have resources relevant to the particular inquiry units are identified in the section titled "Inquiry Units" on page 64. When page numbers are not specified for a given reference, it is suggested that the learners look up relevant information in the reference's table of contents and index. Full reference listings are in the master bibliography at the end of this book.

Handouts for this study guide are

▶ Figure 1, "Self-Diagnostic Rating Scale"

▶ Exhibit 2-2. "Guidelines for Using Learning Contracts"

▶ Exhibit 2-3. "Consultation Exercise."

Process Design

I. Day 1

A. Climate setting; see Exhibit 2-1, "Basic Climate-Setting Exercise" (75 minutes)

1. Small groups share their what's, who's, resources, and concerns.

B. Analysis of this experience and generalizations about the characteristics of a climate that is conducive to learning (45 minutes)

C. Break

D. Self-diagnosis of learning needs (60 minutes)

1. Individual learners turn to Figure 1, "Self-Diagnostic Rating Scale," and rate each competency statement as described at the top of the form. Notice that there are blanks for you to write in additional competencies that you wish to add to the model.

E. Review of self-diagnosed learning needs and consultation exercise (90 minutes)

1. Learners form consultation teams of three each to reality-test one another's self-ratings; see Exhibit 2-3, "Consultation Exercise."

II. Day 2

A. Drafting a learning contract (75 minutes)

1. Learners read Knowles (1980), pp. 382-385; Exhibit 2-2, "Guidelines for Using Learning Contracts"; and Figure 3, "A Learning Contract."

2. Each learner finds those competencies in the self-diagnosis in Figure 1 where the P is two or more notches below the R and translates them into learning objectives in the first column of the learning contract in Figure 3.

3. Learners fill in the remaining columns of the contract according to the guidelines.

B. Break

C. Review of learning contracts (90 minutes)

    1. Learners review their contracts with members of their consultation teams.

D. Break

E. Review the plan of work for this course, with learners raising questions needing clarification (45 minutes)

F. Facilitator identification of needed resources (60 minutes)

    1. Learners pool items in their learning contracts specifying the use of the facilitator's content resources.

G. Break

H. Organization of inquiry teams (30 minutes)

    1. Learners choose one inquiry unit to take special responsibility for.

I. Plan work (90 minutes)

    1. Inquiry teams see Exhibit 2-4, "Suggestions for Inquiry Teams," and Figure 7, "Process Rating Sheet for Inquiry Teams," to plan work.

III. Day 3

A. Progress reports by inquiry teams and scheduling of reports (30 minutes)

B. Presentation of first team (60 minutes)

C. Commentary by facilitator and learners (30 minutes)

D. Break

E. Presentation of second team (60 minutes)

F. Commentary by facilitator and learners (30 minutes)

G. Formative evaluation (30 minutes)

IV. **Day 4**

A. Presentation of third team (60 minutes)

B. Commentary by facilitator and learners (30 minutes)

C. Break

D. Presentation of fourth team (60 minutes)

E. Commentary by facilitator and learners (30 minutes)

F. Break

G. Presentation of fifth team (60 minutes)

H. Commentary by facilitator and learners (30 minutes)

I. Break

J. Presentation of sixth team (60 minutes)

K. Commentary by facilitator and learners (30 minutes)

L. Formative evaluation (45 minutes)

V. **Day 5**

A. Presentation of seventh team (60 minutes)

B. Commentary by facilitator and learners (30 minutes)

C. Break

D. Presentation of eighth team (60 minutes)

E. Commentary by facilitator and learners (30 minutes)

F. Break

G. Presentation of ninth team (60 minutes)

H. Commentary by facilitator and learners (30 minutes)

VI. **Day 6**

A. Presentation of tenth team (60 minutes)

B. Commentary by facilitator and learners (30 minutes)

C. Break

D. Identification of unresolved issues and concerns, with responses by facilitator (75 minutes)

E. Break

F. Review of portfolios of evidence by consultation teams (90 minutes)

G. Break

H. Analysis of the total experience, with generalizations about the program planning process (45 minutes)

I. Input on program evaluation and evaluation of this course (60 minutes)

Inquiry Units

I. **Organizing a program**

A. An overview of the program planning process

—Knowles (1980), chapters 2, 3, 9.
—Houle (1972a), chapter 1.
—Sanders (1966), pp. 94-109, 352-360.

—Knox, et al. (1980), chapters 1-3.

B. Establishing an organizational structure and climate

   1. Philosophy of administration

     —Knowles (1980), chapter 5.
     —Houle (1972a), chapter 2.
     —Knox, et al. (1980), chapter 8.

   2. Policy-making structure

     —Knowles (1980), pp. 70-78.
     —Sanders (1966), pp. 33-47.
     —Houle (1960), pp. 1-167.

C. Determining needs and interests

   1. Individual needs

     —Knowles (1980), chapter 6.
     —Boone, et al. (1980), chapters 1-2.

   2. Organizational needs

     —Knowles (1980), chapter 6.
     —Hospital Research and Educational Trust (1970), chapter 2.

   3. Community and societal needs

     —Knowles (1980), chapter 6.
     —Boone, et al. (1980), chapter 14.

D. Formulating aims and objectives

   —Knowles (1980), chapter 7.
   —Sanders (1966), pp. 417-423.
   —Houle (1972a), chapters 3, 5.
   —Knox, et al. (1980), chapter 3.

II. Designing a program

A. Theory and principles of design

—Knowles (1980), chapter 8.
—Houle (1972a), chapters 3, 5.
—Sanders (1966), pp. 94-104.

B. Selection and scheduling of activities

—Knowles (1980), chapter 8.
—Houle (1972b), pp. 9, 151-152, 160-161.

III. Operating a program

A. Staffing

—Knowles (1980), pp. 78-80.
—Knox, et al. (1980), chapter 7.

B. Recruiting and training leaders and teachers

—Knowles (1980), pp. 156-163.
—Sanders (1966), pp. 315-330, 391-402.

C. Managing facilities and procedures

—Knowles (1980), pp. 163-170.

D. Educational counseling

—Knowles (1980), pp. 133-134, 171-176.

E. Promotion and public relations

—Knowles (1980), pp. 176-189.
—Sanders (1966), pp. 167-232, 375-387.

F. Financing

—Knowles (1980), pp. 190-193.

G. Methods and techniques

—Knowles (1980), chapter 11.
—Knowles and Knowles (1972).
—Houle (1972a), chapter 4.
—Leypoldt (1967).
—Pfeiffer and Jones (1969).

H. Program evaluation

—Knowles (1980), chapter 10.
—Houle (1972a), chapter 4.
—Sanders (1966), pp. 339-351.
—Knox, et al. (1980), chapter 4.
—Patton (1980).
—Patton (1981).
—Patton (1982).

IV. Organizational dynamics, change strategies, and the consultant's role

—Knowles (1980), chapters 2-3.
—Bennis, et al. (1968).
—Schein (1969), pp. 1-147.
—Sanders (1966), pp. 69-86.

❖ Exhibit 3-5. Facilitating Self-Directed Learning ❖

Objectives

The general objectives of this course are to help learners develop or strengthen the following competencies:

▶ an understanding of the modern, andragogical concepts of learning and how these differ from traditional, pedagogical concepts of teaching and learning

▶ knowledge of the role of educator as facilitator and resource for self-directed learners

▶ the ability to apply these concepts to the designing and conducting of learning experiences for a variety of purposes in a variety of settings.

Resources

The basic text is Knowles's *Self-Directed Learning: A Guide for Learners and Teachers* (Follett Press, 1975). Handouts include the following:

▶ Figure 1, "Self-Diagnostic Rating Scale"
▶ Exhibit 2-2, "Guidelines for Using Learning Contracts"
▶ Exhibit 2-3, "Consultation Exercise"
▶ Exhibit 2-4, "Suggestions for Inquiry Teams."

Process Design

I. Day 1

    A. Climate-setting exercise (90 minutes)

        1. Introduce the exercise. Learners read Knowles (1975), pp. 9-11.

        2. Group members share their what's, who's, resources, and concerns. One member volunteers to give a summary report.

        3. The groups' reporters give the summary reports (45 minutes).

    B. Break

C. Inquiry Projects 1 and 2: The why and what of self-directed learning (180 minutes)

    1. Learners read Knowles (1975), pp. 14-22, Learning Resource A.

    2. Groups pool reactions, issues, and questions. One member volunteers to report the collected information.

    3. The facilitator responds to the groups' reports.

II. Day 2

A. Inquiry Project 3: What competencies are required for self-directed learning? (75 minutes)

    1. Learners read Knowles (1975), pp. 23-24.

    2. Learners complete the self-rating scale in Learning Resource B in Knowles (1975), p. 61.

B. Inquiry Project 4: Designing a learning plan (45 minutes)

    1. Learners read Knowles (1975), pp. 25-28.

    2. Learners draft learning contracts for developing needed competencies for self-directed learning, using Figure 3, "A Learning Contract."

C. Break

D. Learners implement their learning contracts, using any resources in the room. (60 minutes)

E. Break

F. The role of the learning facilitator defined and implemented (90 minutes)

    1. Learners read Knowles (1975), pp. 29-58.

2. Groups pool reactions, issues, and questions. One member volunteers to report this information.

3. The facilitator responds to the groups' reports.

G. Break

H. Diagnosis of competency-development needs as a facilitator of learning (60 minutes)

1. Learners rate themselves on the "Self-Diagnostic Rating Scale" in Figure 1.

2. Learners review one another's ratings in teams of two or three.

I. Preparation of learning contracts for the course (60 minutes)

1. Learners read "Guidelines for Using Learning Contracts" in Exhibit 2-2.

2. Each student selects one competency statement in which there is a gap between the R and the P in the "Self-Diagnostic Rating Scale," translates it into a learning objective, and completes the columns in the learning contract for that objective.

3. Students raise questions about the contracting process for the facilitator to respond to.

4. Students will bring completed contracts to the next meeting.

III. Day 3

A. Peer review of learning contracts in "Consultation Exercise" in Exhibit 2-3 (120 minutes)

1. Learners read Knowles (1975), pp. 75-80.

2. Groups form triads, with one member presenting his or her contract for review by a second member (the consultant),

while a third member observes. Each round lasts 30 minutes.

3. Groups analyze this experience; see Knowles (1975), p. 78r.

B. Break

C. Clinic on problems and issues regarding contract learning (30 minutes)

D. Organization of learning groups around contract objectives (45 minutes)

E. Learning groups read "Suggestions for Inquiry Teams" in Exhibit 2-4 and then meet (75 minutes)

IV. **Day 4**

A. Learning groups meet (120 minutes)

B. Break

C. Learning groups meet (75 minutes)

D. Break

E. Learning groups report (90 minutes)

F. Break

G. Identification of back-home application projects (30 minutes)

H. Organization of back-home application teams (30 minutes)

I. Back-home application teams meet (60 minutes)

V. **Days 5 to 18**

A. Learners prepare portfolios of evidence of accomplishment of objectives

VI. Day 19

A. Back-home application teams meet (120 minutes)

B. Break

C. Back-home application teams meet (120 minutes)

D. Clinic on problems and issues of back-home application teams (90 minutes)

VII. Day 20

A. Consultation triads review portfolios of evidence (120 minutes)

B. Break

C. Consultation teams fill out grade reports for each student. Learners polish portfolios of evidence and turn them in to the facilitator. (75 minutes)

D. Break

E. Mop-up of unresolved issues and questions regarding self-directed learning (60 minutes)

F. Course evaluation (60 minutes)

❖ Exhibit 3-6. Training and the Applied Behavioral Sciences ❖

Assumptions

This study guide is based on the assumption that learning is an internal process, with the locus of control of that process residing in the learner, but one that can be facilitated by outside helpers. It further assumes that certain conditions are more conducive to learning than others, and that these superior conditions are produced by learning-teaching practices that adhere to superior principles of teaching. These conditions and principles are described in Knowles's *The Modern Practice of Adult Education: From Pedagogy to Andragogy* (Follett Press, 1980), pp. 57-58.

This study guide is based on certain assumptions about adults as learners and the learning process. These assumptions have some implications for what you do and how you will use the facilitator, your peers, and the resource materials. First, it assumes that you as a learner

▶ have the self-concept of being an adult and the desire and capability of taking responsibility for planning and managing your own learning with help from fellow students, the facilitator, and other helpers. It further assumes that what you learn through your own initiative you will learn more effectively than what you learn through imposition by others.

▶ bring with you into this activity a rich background of experience that is a valuable resource both for your own learning and for the learning of fellow students. It further assumes that your experience is different from the experience of other members of the course, and that your combined experiences represent a rich pool of resources for one another's learning.

▶ are readiest to learn those things you perceive will help you perform more effectively in your life tasks and allow you to achieve a higher level of potential. It further assumes that the study guide and the facilitator have an obligation to help you see how the course can help you perform more effectively.

▶ are unique, along with every other member of the course, with your own styles and paces of learning, outside commitments and pressures, goals, and internal motivations. It also assumes that your learning plans and strategies must be highly individualized.

Objectives

This course will help learners develop or strengthen the following competencies:

 ▶ basic knowledge and understanding of the modern concepts and research findings from the behavioral sciences regarding the needs, interests, motivations, capacities, and developmental processes of adult learners

 ▶ an understanding of the differences in assumptions about youths and adults as learners and the implications of these differences for teaching and training

 ▶ knowledge of the various theories of learning and the ability to assess their relevance to particular adult-learning situations

 ▶ the ability to conceptualize and perform the role of teacher-trainer as a facilitator and resource person for self-directed learners

 ▶ knowledge of the basic principles and methods of program development and an understanding of their application in a variety of settings

 ▶ skill in the basic functions of program management, such as policy formulation; selecting, training, and supervising leaders and teachers; promoting and interpreting programs; financing; working with boards and committees; and program evaluation

 ▶ an understanding of a broad range of methods and techniques available to help adults learn and become skilled in using these methods and techniques

 ▶ knowledge of the rationale for selecting particular methods and techniques for achieving particular educational objectives

 ▶ skill in designing learning experiences that use combinations of methods and techniques for optimal learning

 ▶ insight into the nature and dynamics of organizational life and an understanding of the implications of these dynamics for the management of an adult educational enterprise

 ▶ an understanding of the role of adult educator as a consultant and skill in using the consultation process in facilitating personal, group, and organizational change.

Requirements for accomplishing this course's purpose will vary according to the prior learning of the participants. Each learner will engage in a self-diagnostic process using the "Self-Diagnostic Rating Scale" in Figure 1. Each person will then construct, with the facilitator's help, a learning contract containing as objectives those abilities that are not yet achieved at a high level of competence. Those learners who wish to contract for a "B" grade need to include in their contract only the objectives listed at the beginning of this study guide that they have not yet achieved at the required level. Those learners wishing to contract for an "A" grade must submit a separate contract specifying one or more objectives that will ensure superior performance and will build on their unique strengths, talents, interests, and career goals. You may prepare in advance for entering into this contracting process by reading Knowles's *Self-Directed Learning: A Guide for Learners and Teachers* (Follett Press, 1975).

Resources

This course uses the following basic references:

Cross, P.K. *Adults as Learners.* Jossey-Bass Publishers, 1981.

Knowles, Malcolm S. *The Modern Practice of Adult Education: From Pedagogy to Andragogy.* Follett Press, 1980.

—. *The Adult Learner: A Neglected Species.* Gulf Publishing Co., 1984b.

—. *Self-Directed Learning: A Guide for Learners and Teachers.* Follett Press, 1975.

Nadler, L. *The Handbook of Human Resource Development.* John Wiley & Sons Inc., 1984.

Handouts used in this course are:
▶ Figure 1, "Self-Diagnostic Rating Scale"
▶ Exhibit 2-2, "Guidelines for Using Learning Contracts"
▶ Exhibit 2-3, "Consultation Exercise"
▶ Exhibit 2-4, "Suggestions for Inquiry Teams."

Process Design
I.   Day 1

A. Climate setting; see Exhibit 2-1, "Basic Climate-Setting Exercise" (60 minutes)

1. Small groups share their what's, who's, resources, and concerns.

B. Analysis of this experience and generalizations about the characteristics of a climate that is conducive to learning (30 minutes)

C. Break

D. The facilitator's theoretical framework and the definition of his or her role (60 minutes)

1. A dialogic self-revelation

E. Break

F. Self-diagnosis of learning needs (60 minutes)

1. Individual learners turn to Figure 1, "Self-Diagnostic Rating Scale," and rate themselves on each competency statement described at the top of the form. Notice that there are blanks for the learners to write in additional competencies that they wish to add to the model.

G. Review of self-diagnosed learning needs (30 minutes)

1. Learners form consultation teams of three or four each and reality-test one another's self-ratings.

H. Break

I. Drafting a learning contract (60 minutes)

1. Learners read Exhibit 2-2, "Guidelines for Using Learning Contracts." Each learner then turns to his or her own self-diagnosis, identifies those competency statements in which the P is two or more notches below the R, and translates them into learning objectives in the first column of the learning contract in Figure 3. They fill in the remaining columns of the contract form in accordance with the guidelines.

II. Day 2

A. Continue drafting the learning contract (45 minutes)

B. Analysis of the contracting process, and discussion of questions, problems, and concerns about it (30 minutes)

C. Break

D. Review of learning contracts and consultation exercise (75 minutes)

1. Learners review their contracts with members of their consultation team while doing the consultation exercise in Exhibit 2-3.

E. Break

F. Continue review of learning contracts (30 minutes)

G. Analysis of this experience (15 minutes)

1. What behaviors of the consultants facilitate or inhibit getting the desired help?

H. Review of this course's plan of work (30 minutes)

1. Learners raise questions needing clarification.

I. Break

J. Review of inquiry units (15 minutes)

K. Selection of inquiry teams and first meetings (60 minutes)

1. Learners choose one inquiry unit to take special responsibility for.

2. Inquiry teams meet to plan work. See Exhibit 2-4, "Suggestions for Inquiry Teams."

III. Day 3

A. Inquiry teams meet, with facilitator as a roving consultant (75 minutes)

B. Break

C. Inquiry teams meet (75 minutes)

D. Break

E. Inquiry-team progress reports (45 minutes)

F. Inquiry teams meet (45 minutes)

G. Break

H. Inquiry teams pool items in their contracts specifying the use of the facilitator's content resources and propose agenda items for Day 4 (60 minutes)

IV. Day 4

A. Execution of plans made on the afternoon of Day 3, with a short break in the middle (165 minutes)

B. Break

C. Inquiry teams meet to plan work (90 minutes)

　　1. Inquiry teams propose time schedules for their reports.

D. Break

E. Progress reports and time schedule proposals from inquiry teams; final planning for sessions (60 minutes)

V. Day 5

A. Reports of scheduled inquiry teams, with commentary by facilitator and learners after each one and a short break in the middle of the session (165 minutes)

B. Break

C. Reports of scheduled inquiry teams, with a short break in the middle of the session (165 minutes)

VI. Day 6

A. Reports of scheduled inquiry teams, with commentary by facilitator and learners following each and a short break in the middle of the session (165 minutes)

B. Break

C. Reports of scheduled inquiry teams, with a short break in the middle of the session (165 minutes)

VII. Day 7

A. Reports of scheduled inquiry teams, with commentary by facilitator and learners following each and a short break in the middle of the session (165 minutes)

B. Break

C. Reports of scheduled inquiry teams, with a short break in the middle of the session (165 minutes)

VIII. Day 8

A. Review of portfolios of evidence by consultation teams (75 minutes)

B. Break

C. Continuation of review of portfolios of evidence by consultation teams (75 minutes)

D. Pairs of consultation teams pool unresolved issues and concerns (30 minutes)

E. Break

F. Groups report unresolved issues and concerns (15 minutes)

G. Facilitator responds to unresolved issues and concerns (75 minutes)

H. Break

I. Learners evaluate this course (60 minutes)

Inquiry Units
I. Unit 1

A. Adult learning and teaching

1. What are the unique characteristics of adults as learners with respect to their needs, interests, motivations, capacities, and developmental processes?

—Cross (1981), pp. 50-186.
—Knowles (1980), pp. 40-60.
—Knowles (1984a) pp. 27-63.
—Knowles (1984b), pp. 6-12.
—Knox (1977), pp. 1-31, 171-244, 405-469, 551-578.
—Wlodkowski (1985), pp. 1-15, 44-71.

2. What are the differences in assumptions about youths and adults as learners, and what are the implications of these differences for teaching and training?

—Knowles (1980), pp. 43-60.
—Nadler (1984), sections 6.1-6.22.

3. What are the various theories of learning and their relevance to particular learning situations?

—Cross (1981), pp. 220-252.
—Knowles (1984a), pp. 1-26, 64-139.

4. What is the role of a teacher or trainer as a facilitator and re-source person for self-directed learners?

—Knowles (1975), pp. 29-58.
—Knowles (1980), pp. 24-39.
—Knowles (1984a), pp. 189-200.
—Knowles (1984b), pp. 141-146.
—Wlodkowski (1985), pp. 16-43, 72-280.

II. Unit 2

A. Program development

1. What are the basic principles and methods of program devel-opment in human resources development and what are their applications in a variety of settings? What is the role of the human resource developer?

—Boone (1985), pp. 1-78.
—Knowles (1980), pp. 66-154.
—Nadler (1970), pp. 147-247, 1-40.
—Nadler (1984), sections 7.1-7.35.

2. What are the tasks and skills required to perform the basic functions of program management?

—Boone (1985), pp. 79-206.
—Knowles (1980), pp. 155-218.
—Nadler (1970), pp. 41-123.

III. Unit 3

A. Methods and techniques

1. What is the broad range of methods and techniques available to help adults learn and what skills are required to use them?

Which methods and techniques are effective for achieving particular objectives?

—Craig (1976), sections 32.3-47.16.
—Knowles (1980), pp. 222-249.
—Nadler (1980), pp. 94-107.
—Nadler (1984), sections 8.1-11.32.

2. How can learning experiences be designed to use combinations of methods and techniques for optimal learning?

—Knowles (1984a), pp. 106-139, 177-188.

IV. Unit 4

A. The organization as a system of learning resources

1. What are the dynamics of organizational life that affect the management of adult educational or training systems?

—Craig (1976), pp. 8.3-8.8, 8.26.
—Knowles (1980), pp. 66-81.
—Knowles (1984a), pp. 192-200, 228-234.
—Nadler (1980), pp. 124-161.
—Nadler (1984), sections 2.1-2.15, 4.1-4.26.

2. What is the role of the human resource developer as a consultant in facilitating personal, group, and organizational change, and what skills are involved?

—Argyris (1970).
—Bennis, Benne, and Chin (1968).
—Lippitt (1973).
—Lippitt and Lippitt (1978).
—Nadler (1970), pp. 232-247.
—Nadler (1984), sections 5.1-5.27.
—Schein (1969).

CHAPTER 4

Designs for Workshops

My basic design for workshops is presented in Exhibit 4-1, "One-Day Workshop: Understanding and Working With Adult Learners." I have adapted this design to a half-day workshop (three-and-a-half hours long) by

- condensing the climate-setting exercise to 20 minutes by having the learners get acquainted by name, position, and organization in their small groups
- reducing the presentation of the theoretical framework of andragogy to 15 minutes by having the learners examine the chart "Assumptions and Process Elements of the Pedagogical and Andragogical Models of Learning" in Figure 8
- shortening the time for drafting learning contracts to 30 minutes by eliminating the peer review in triads)
- limiting the problem clinic to whatever time is left over
- suggesting that learners mail me their evaluations of the workshop.

I distribute copies of Figure 8, "Assumptions and Process Elements of the Pedagogical and Andragogical Models of Learning," and ask the learners to take about five minutes to examine the assumptions on the left side and then the process elements on the right side. I then ask them to get into their groups of four or five and share questions they have about the meaning of the charts. One group member volunteers to serve as the reporter for the group. Then I invite each reporter to ask one of these questions, and I respond. After all reporters have asked one question, I open the floor to any additional questions. During my responses, I frequently invite additional ideas from any of the learners. This session usually turns out to be very dialogic.

I also adapt this basic design to one-and-a-half- and two-day workshops, as shown in Exhibit 4-2, "One-and-One-Half-Day Workshop: Facilitating Adult Learning in HRD."

In this chapter:

❖ Exhibit 4-1. One-Day Workshop: Understanding and Working With Adult Learners ❖

Objectives

The general objectives of the workshop are to help learners develop or strengthen the following competencies:

- ▶ an understanding of the modern concepts of adult learning and how these differ from traditional concepts of youth learning
- ▶ an understanding of the role of educator as facilitator and resource for self-directed learners
- ▶ the ability to apply these concepts to the designing of learning experiences for yourself and others through the use of learning contracts.

Resources

The following handouts should be used in this one-day workshop:

- ▶ Figure 1, "Self-Diagnostic Rating Scale"
- ▶ Figure 8, "Assumptions and Process Elements of the Pedagogical and Andragogical Models of Learning"
- ▶ Exhibit 2-2, "Guidelines for Using Learning Contracts"
- ▶ Exhibit 2-3, "Consultation Exercise."

Process Design

I. Day 1

A. Climate-setting exercise (60 minutes)

1. Learners share information in small groups about their what's, who's, questions, problems, or issues.

B. Analysis of this experience and identification of the characteristics of a climate that is conducive to learning (15 minutes)

C. Break

D. Dialogic presentation of the theoretical framework of andragogy; see Figure 8, "Assumptions and Process Elements of the Pedagogical and Andragogical Models of Learning" (60 minutes)

E. Introduction to competency-based education and a model of competencies for a facilitator of learning; see Figure 1, "Self-Diagnostic Rating Scale" (30 minutes)

F. Break

G. Diagnosis of competency-development needs by learners (30 minutes)

H. Drafting of learning contracts (60 minutes)

   1. Facilitator introduces contract learning; see Exhibit 2-2, "Guidelines for Using Learning Contracts."

   2. Learners draft contracts for two or three high-priority learning objectives.

   3. Learners review contracts in triads; see Exhibit 2-3, "Consultation Exercise."

I. Break

J. Problem clinic (45 minutes)

   1. Facilitator responds to questions about this process and any unresolved problems and issues.

K. Evaluation of this workshop (30 minutes)

❖ Exhibit 4-2. One-and-One-Half-Day Workshop: Facilitating Adult Learning in HRD ❖

Objectives

The basic objectives of this one-and-one-half-day workshop are to provide resources to help learners develop or strengthen the following competencies:

- an understanding of the modern concepts of adult learning and how these differ from traditional concepts of youth learning
- an understanding of the role of educator as facilitator and resource for self-directed learners
- the ability to apply these concepts to the designing of learning experiences for themselves and others through the use of learning contracts.

Resources

The following handouts should be used in this workshop:

- Figure 1, "Self-Diagnostic Rating Scale"
- Figure 8, "Assumptions and Process Elements of the Pedagogical and Andragogical Models of Learning"
- Exhibit 2-1, "Basic Climate-Setting Exercise"
- Exhibit 2-2, "Guidelines for Using Learning Contracts"
- Exhibit 2-3, "Consultation Exercise."

Process Design

I. **Day 1**

A. Climate setting and problem census; see Exhibit 2-1, "Basic Climate-Setting Exercise" (60 minutes)

B. Analysis of this experience and exploration of the characteristics of a climate that is conducive to learning (30 minutes)

C. Break

D. Dialogic presentation of the theoretical framework of andragogy; see Figure 8, "Assumptions and Process Elements of the Pedagogical and Andragogical Models of Learning" (75 minutes)

E. Break

F. Self-diagnosis of competency-development needs; see Figure 1, "Self-Diagnostic Rating Scale" (45 minutes)

II. Day 2

A. Introduction to contract learning; see Exhibit 2-2, "Guidelines for Using Learning Contracts" (30 minutes)

B. Drafting of learning contracts (45 minutes)

C. Break

D. Review of learning contracts in consultation triads via exercise in giving and receiving help; see Exhibit 2-3, "Consultation Exercise" (60 minutes)

E. Analysis of the role of facilitator and resource person (30 minutes)

F. Break

G. Questions and answers regarding competency-based education, self-diagnosis of learning needs, and contract learning (45 minutes)

H. Identification of unresolved questions, problems, and issues in small groups (30 minutes)

I. Problem clinic with facilitator as resource (30 minutes)

J. Break

K. Continuation of problem clinic (30 minutes)

L. Conceptualization of an organization as a system of learning resources and of human resources development as managing a system of learning resources (30 minutes)

M. Evaluation of this workshop (15 minutes)

Figure 8. Assumptions and Process Elements of the Pedagogical and Andragogical Models of Learning

The body of theory and practice on which teacher-directed learning is based is often given the label "pedagogy," from the Greek words *paid* (meaning child) and *agogus* (meaning guide or leader). This is defined as the art and science of teaching children.

The body of theory and practice on which self-directed learning is based is labeled "andragogy," from the Greek word *aner* (meaning adult) and *agogus*. This is defined as the art and science of helping adults—or even better, maturing human beings—learn.

These two models do not represent bad/good or child/adult dichotomies, but rather a continuum of assumptions to be checked out in terms of their appropriateness for particular learners in particular situations. If a pedagogical assumption is realistic for a particular situation, then pedagogical strategies are appropriate. For example, if a learner is entering into a totally new content area, he or she will be dependent on a teacher until enough content has been acquired to enable self-directed inquiry to begin.

Assumptions About...	Pedagogical	Andragogical
Concept of the learner	Dependent personality	Increasingly self-directing
Role of learner's experience	To be built on, rather than used as a resource	A rich resource for learning by self and others
Readiness to learn	Uniform by age level and curriculum	Develops from life tasks and problems
Orientation to learning	Subject-centered	Task- or problem-centered
Motivation	By external rewards and punishment	By internal incentives and curiosity

Figure 8 (continued). Assumptions and Process Elements of the Pedagogical and Andragogical Models of Learning

Process Elements	Pedagogical	Andragogical
Climate	Tense, low trust Formal, cold, aloof Authority-oriented Competitive, judgmental	Relaxed, trusting Mutually respectful Informal, warm Collaborative, supportive
Planning	Primarily by teacher	Mutually by learners and facilitator
Diagnosis of needs	Primarily by teacher	By mutual assessment
Setting of objectives	Primarily by teacher	By mutual negotiation
Designing learning plans	Teacher's content plans Course syllabus Logical sequence	Learning contracts Learning projects Sequenced by readiness
Learning activities	Transmittal techniques Assigned readings	Inquiry projects Independent study Experiential techniques
Evaluation	By teacher Norm-referenced (on a curve) With grades	By learner-collected evidence validated by peers, facilitators, and experts Criterion-referenced

CHAPTER 5

Designs for Conference Sessions, "Lectures," and Keynote Speeches

I am frequently asked to make short presentations of approximately one hour at conferences, university courses, and organizational meetings. I feel an obligation to be faithful to my andragogical model—that is, to involve the audiences in a process of active inquiry—even in these circumstances, particularly because all of my presentations have to do with some aspect of adult education or human resource development.

Perhaps my most frequent assignment is to give a talk on the future of such entities as education, adult education, higher education, nontraditional education, workplace training, human resource development, and the like. My most common audiences are university faculties, continuing education directors, and chapter members of the American Society for Training and Development at their monthly meetings. Sponsors give these sessions such descriptive labels as "inductive lectures," "dialogic lectures," and "participatory sessions"—if they label them at all. More often, they let the learners be surprised. Fortunately, the surprise turns out to be pleasant for most of them.

My typical design for a one-hour session on the future of adult education is as follows.

After being introduced, I repeat the title and point out that professional futurists use two techniques for looking into the future:

▶ scenario writing, in which they dream about what they would like the future to be like—say in the year 2020—and write a scenario describing it

▶ forecasting, in which they identify current trends and project these into the future.

I explain that I would like to share responsibility with the learners for

---

peering into the crystal ball at adult education in 2020.

I then ask them to form small groups by turning their chairs so that they face three or four neighbors and brainstorm what they would like to see come into being in adult education in the next few decades. I ask one member of each group to volunteer to be the reporter for his or her group to give a summary of the ideas generated.

I give them 15 minutes to share their dreams. Then I call on the reporters to give their reports. Typically, the reports include such ideas as:

- ▶ Adult education has become the largest segment of the national educational enterprise.
- ▶ More people are participating in adult education programs than in all elementary, secondary, and higher education programs combined.
- ▶ Most adult students are studying at home or at work through computer networks or interactive television.
- ▶ All teachers have been retrained to be mentors or facilitators rather than instructors.
- ▶ College dormitories have become more like motels, serving adult students in one- to five-day workshops and seminars.
- ▶ Didactic courses have been replaced by competency-based, self-directed learning projects, and grades have been replaced by performance assessments.

When at least a representative sample of reports have been completed I say, "I am happy to assure you that most of these dreams are going to come true, as you will see when I pick up on current trends and project them into the future, revealing what it is really going to be like in 2020." I build on the following major trends:

- ▶ The demographic revolution guarantees that we will be dealing with an increasingly aging and diversified population—and therefore with an aging workforce that will need continuous retraining.
- ▶ The accelerating pace of change from the knowledge revolution, the technological revolution, and the information society will require that we provide not only lifelong educational opportunities but training in the skills of personal change.
- ▶ An explosive infusion of research-based knowledge about the nature of learning (particularly adult learning) will require us to shift emphasis in adult education from teaching to self-directed learning.
- ▶ The rapid development of new forms of electronic media for the delivery of educational services and resources will make it possible

for us to make learning experiences available to learners at their convenience in terms of time, place, and pace.

If there is still some time remaining, I open the session to questions and comments.

If the topic is something other than the future—such as improving patient education, lifelong learning, responding to adult developmental and learning needs, improving quality through learning, or a host of other topics—I use an adaptation of this basic design. I open the session by explaining that I wish to demonstrate learning as a process of active inquiry. I then put participants into small groups for a few minutes to generate questions about the topic that they would like me to talk with them about. Then I respond to the questions as they are raised.

Bibliography

Alford, H.J. *Continuing Education in Action.* New York: John Wiley & Sons Inc., 1968.

Arends, R.I., and J.H. Arends. *Systems Change Strategies in Educational Settings.* New York: Human Sciences Press, 1977.

Argyris, C. *Intervention Theory and Method: A Behavioral Science View.* Reading, MA: Addison-Wesley Publishing Co., 1970.

Axford, R.W. *Adult Education: The Open Door.* Scranton, PA: International Textbook Co., 1969.

Baltes, P.D. (ed.) *Life-Span Development and Behavior.* New York: Academic Press, 1978.

Bandura, A. *Principles of Behavior Modification.* New York: Holt, Rinehart & Winston, 1969.

Barker, Roger G. *Ecological Psychology: Concepts and Methods for Studying the Environment of Human Behavior.* Stanford, CA: Stanford University Press, 1968.

—, et al. *Habitats, Environments, and Human Behavior.* San Francisco: Jossey-Bass Publishers, 1978.

Barrett, J.H. *Individual Goals and Organizational Objectives.* Ann Arbor: Institute of Social Research, University of Michigan, 1970.

Benne, K., L. Bradford, and R. Lippitt. *The Laboratory Method of Changing and Learning.* Palo Alto, CA: Science and Behavior Books, 1975.

Bennis, W., K. Benne, and R. Chin. *The Planning of Change.* New York: Holt, Rinehart & Winston, 1968.

Bergevin, P.E. *A Philosophy for Adult Education.* New York: Seabury Press, 1967.

Birren, F. *Light, Color, and Environment.* New York: Van Nostrand Reinhold, 1969.

Bischof, L.J. *Adult Psychology.* New York: Harper & Row Publishers, 1969.

Blakely, R.J. *The New Environment: Questions for Adult Educators.* Syracuse, NY: Syracuse University, 1971.

—. *Toward a Homeodynamic Society.* Syracuse, NY: Syracuse University, 1965.

Boocock, S.S. *An Introduction to the Sociology of Learning.* Boston: Houghton Mifflin Co., 1972.

Boone, E.J. *Developing Programs in Adult Education.* Englewood Cliffs, NJ: Prentice-Hall, 1985.

—, et al. *Serving Personal and Community Needs Through Adult Education.* San Francisco: Jossey-Bass Publishers, 1980.

Botkin, J.W., et al. *No Limits to Learning.* New York: Pergamon Press, 1979.

Botwinick, J. *Cognitive Processes in Maturity and Old Age.* New York: Springer Publishing Co., 1967.

Bronfenbrenner, U. *The Ecology of Human Development.* Cambridge, MA: Harvard University Press, 1979.

Brunner, E. *An Overview of Adult Education Research.* Washington, DC: Adult Education Association, 1959.

Charters, A.N. *Toward the Educative Society.* Syracuse, NY: Syracuse University, 1971.

Commission on Non-Traditional Study. *Diversity by Design.* San Francisco: Jossey-Bass Publishers, 1973.

Cook, S.D., et al. *Dilemmas of American Policy: Crucial Issues in Contemporary Society.* Syracuse, NY: Syracuse University, 1969.

Craig, R.L. (ed.) *Training and Development Handbook.* New York: McGraw-Hill Publishing Co., 1976.

Cross, K.P. *Adults as Learners.* San Francisco: Jossey-Bass Publishers, 1981.

Cross, P. *Accent on Learning.* San Francisco: Jossey-Bass Publishers, 1976.

Dave, R.H. (ed.) *Reflections of Lifelong Education and the School.* Hamburg, Germany: UNESCO Institute for Education, 1975.

David, T.G., and B.D. Wright (eds.) *Learning Environments.* Chicago: University of Chicago Press, 1975.

Davis, G.A., and J.A. Scott. *Training Creative Thinking.* New York: Holt, Rinehart & Winston, 1971.

A Design for Democracy, a report of the Adult Education Committee of the British Ministry of Reconstruction. New York: Association Press, 1956.

Deutsch, M., et al. (eds.) *Social Class, Race, and Psychological Development.* New York: Holt, Rinehart & Winston, 1968.

Draves, W. *The Free University.* Chicago: Follett Press, 1980.

Erickson, E.H. *Identity and the Life Cycle.* New York: International Universities Press, 1959.

Etzioni, A. *Complex Organizations.* New York: Free Press, 1961.

—. *A Sociological Reader on Complex Organizations*. New York: Holt, Rinehart & Winston, 1969.

Faire, E., et al. *Learning To Be: The World of Education Today and Tomorrow*. Paris: UNESCO, 1972.

Freire, P. *Pedagogy of the Oppressed*. New York: Seabury Press, 1970.

Gage, N.L. *Teacher Effectiveness and Teacher Education*. Palo Alto, CA: Pacific Books, 1972.

Gagne, R.M. *The Conditions of Learning*. New York: Holt, Rinehart & Winston, 1965.

Gould, S. *Diversity by Design*. San Francisco: Jossey-Bass Publishers, 1973.

Goulet, L.R., and P.B. Baltes. *Life-Span Developmental Psychology*. New York: Academic Press, 1970.

Grattan, C.H. *In Quest of Knowledge*. New York: Association Press, 1955.

—. *American Ideas About Adult Education, 1710-1951*. New York: Columbia University, 1959.

Greiner, L.E. (ed.) *Organizational Change and Development*. Homewood, IL: Richard D. Irwin Inc., 1971.

Havighurst, R. *Developmental Tasks and Education*. New York: David McKay Co., 1972.

Herzberg, F. *Work and the Nature of Man*. Cleveland: World Publishing Co., 1966.

Hilgard, E.R., and G.H. Bower. *Theories of Learning*. New York: Appleton-Century-Crofts, 1966.

Hornstein, H.A., et al. *Social Intervention*. New York: Free Press, 1971.

Hospital Research and Educational Trust. *Training and Continuing Education: A Handbook for Healthcare*. Chicago: Hospital Research and Educational Trust, 1970.

Houle, Cyril O. *The Design of Education*. San Francisco: Jossey-Bass Publishers, 1972a.

—. *The Effective Board*. New York: Association Press, 1960.

—. *The External Degree*. San Francisco: Jossey-Bass Publishers, 1972b.

—. *The Inquiring Mind*. Madison: University of Wisconsin Press, 1961.

Howe, Michael. *Adult Learning*. New York: John Wiley & Sons Inc., 1977.

Ingalls, J.D. *Human Energy*. Reading, MA: Addison-Wesley Publishing Co., 1976.

—, and J.M. Arceri. *A Trainer's Guide to Andragogy*. Washington, DC: U.S. Department of Health, Education, and Welfare, 1972.

Johnstone, John, and R.J. Rivera. *Volunteers for Learning: A Study of the Educational Pursuits of American Adults*. Chicago: Aldine Publishing Co., 1965.

Keeton, M.T. *Experiential Learning: Rationale, Characteristics, and Assessment*. San Francisco: Jossey-Bass Publishers, 1976.

Kempfer, Homer. *Adult Education*. New York: McGraw-Hill Publishing Co., 1955.

Kidd, J.R. *How Adults Learn*. Chicago: Follett Press, 1973.

Knowles, Malcolm S. *Andragogy in Action*. San Francisco: Jossey-Bass Publishers, 1984a.

— (ed.). *Handbook of Adult Education in the United States*. Washington,

DC: Adult Education Association, 1960.

—. *Informal Adult Education.* New York: Association Press, 1950.

—. *The Adult Education Movement in the United States.* Melbourne, FL: Krieger Publishing Co., 1977.

—. *The Adult Learner: A Neglected Species,* 3d edition. Houston: Gulf Publishing Co., 1984b.

—. *The Modern Practice of Adult Education: From Pedagogy to Andragogy.* Chicago: Follett Press, 1980.

—. *Self-Directed Learning: A Guide for Learners and Teachers.* Chicago: Follett Press, 1975.

—, and Hulda F. Knowles. *Introduction to Group Dynamics.* Chicago: Follett Press, 1972.

Knox, A.B. *Adult Development and Learning.* San Francisco: Jossey-Bass Publishers, 1977.

—, and Associates. *Developing, Administering, and Evaluating Adult Education.* San Francisco: Jossey-Bass Publishers, 1980.

Kuhlen, R. *Psychological Backgrounds of Adult Education.* Brookline, MA: Center for the Study of Liberal Education for Adults, 1964.

Levinson, D.J. *The Seasons of a Man's Life.* New York: Alfred A. Knopf Inc., 1978.

Lewis, K. *Field Theory in Social Science.* New York: Harper & Row Publishers, 1951.

Leypoldt, M. *Forty Ways To Teach in Groups.* Valley Forge, PA: Judson Press, 1967.

Lidz, T. *The Person: His Development Throughout the Life Cycle.* New York: Basic Books, 1968.

Lindeman, Eduard. *The Democratic Man: Selected Writings*, Robert Gessner (ed.). Boston: Beacon Press, 1956.

—. *The Meaning of Adult Education.* New York: New Republic Press, 1926.

Lippit, G. *Organizational Renewal.* New York: Appleton-Century-Crofts, 1969.

—. *Visualizing Change.* Fairfax, VA: NTL Learning Resources, 1973.

—, and R. Lippitt. *The Consulting Process in Action.* La Jolla, CA: University Associates, 1978.

Lorge, I., et al. *Psychology of Adults.* Washington, DC: Adult Education Association, 1963.

Martorana, S.V., and E. Kuhns. *Managing Academic Change.* San Francisco: Jossey-Bass Publishers, 1975.

Maslow, A. *The Farther Reaches of Human Nature.* New York: Viking, 1971.

—. *Motivation and Personality.* New York: Harper & Row Publishers, 1970.

—. *Toward a Psychology of Being.* Princeton, NJ: Van Nostrand Reinhold, 1962.

Miles, M.W., and W.W. Charters, Jr. *Learning in Social Settings.* Boston: Allyn & Bacon Inc., 1970.

Miller, H.L. *Teaching and Learning in Adult Education.* New York: Macmillan Publishing Co., 1964.

Moos, R.H. *Evaluating Educational Environments.* San Francisco: Jossey-Bass Publishers, 1979.

—. *The Human Context: Environmental Determinants of Behavior.* New York: Wiley Interscience, 1976.

—, and P.M. Insel. *Issues in Social Ecology*. Palo Alto, CA: National Press Books, 1974.

Nadler, L. *Corporate Human Resources*. New York: Van Nostrand Reinhold, 1980.

—. *Developing Human Resources*. Houston, TX: Gulf Publishing Co., 1970.

—. *The Handbook of Human Resource Development*. New York: John Wiley & Sons Inc., 1984.

—, and Z. Nadler. *The Conference Book*. Houston: Gulf Publishing Co., 1977.

Neugarten, B.L. (ed.) *Middle Age and Aging*. Chicago: University of Chicago Press, 1968.

—. *Personality in Middle and Later Life*. New York: Atherton Press, 1964.

Patton, M.Q. *Creative Evaluation*. Beverly Hills, CA: Sage Publication Inc., 1981.

—. *Practical Evaluation*. Beverly Hills, CA: Sage Publication Inc., 1982.

—. *Qualitative Evaluation*. Beverly Hills, CA: Sage Publication Inc., 1980.

Pfeiffer, William J., and John E. Jones. *A Handbook of Structured Experiences for Human Relations Training*. San Diego: University Associates, 1969.

Powell, John Walker. *Learning Comes of Age*. New York: Association Press, 1956.

Pressy, S.L., and R.G. Kuhlen. *Psychological Development Through the Life Span*. New York: Harper & Row Publishers, 1957.

Ray, W.S. *Simple Experiments in Psychology*. New York: Behavioral Publications, 1973.

Rogers, C.R. *Client-Centered Therapy: Its Current Practice, Implications, and Theory*. Boston: Houghton Mifflin Co., 1951.

Rogers, C.A. *On Becoming a Person*. Boston: Houghton Mifflin Co., 1961.

—. *Freedom To Learn*. Columbus, OH: Merrill Publishing Co., 1969.

—. *A Way of Being*. Boston: Hougton Mifflin Co., 1980.

Sanders, H.C. (ed.) *The Cooperative Extension Service*. Englewood Cliffs, NJ: Prentice-Hall, 1966.

Schein, E. *Personal and Organizational Change Through Group Methods*. New York: John Wiley & Sons Inc., 1964.

—. *Process Consultation: Its Role in Organization Development*. Reading, MA: Addison-Wesley Publishing Co., 1969.

Sheats, Paul H., Clarence Jayne, and Ralph B. Spence. *Adult Education: The Community Approach*. New York: Dryden Press, 1953.

Sheehy, G. *Passages*. New York: E.P. Dutton, 1974.

Silberman, M.L., J.S. Allender, and J.M. Yanoff. *The Psychology of Open Teaching and Learning: An Inquiry Approach*. Boston: Little, Brown & Co., 1972.

Sillars, Robertson (ed.) *Seeking Common Ground*. Chicago: Adult Education Association, 1958.

Smith, Robert M., George F. Aker, and J.R. Kidd. *Handbook of Adult Education*. New York: Macmillan Publishing Co., 1970.

Stevens-Long, J. *Adult Life: Development Processes*. Palo Alto, CA: Mayfield Publishing Co., 1979.

Tough, Allen. *Learning Without a Teacher.* Toronto: Ontario Institute for Studies in Education, 1967.

—. *The Adult's Learning Projects,* 2d edition. Toronto: Ontario Institute for Studies in Education, 1979.

—. *Intentional Changes.* Chicago: Follett Press, 1982.

Verner, Coolie. *Adult Education.* Washington, DC: Center for Applied Research in Education, 1964.

Wlodkowski, R.J. *Enhancing Adult Motivation To Learn.* San Francisco: Jossey-Bass Publishers, 1985.

Zurcher, L.A. *The Mutable Self: A Concept for Social Change.* Beverly Hills, CA: Sage Publications Inc., 1977.